Sportin'
a 'Tude

Sportin' a 'Tude

Patsy Clairmont

SPORTIN' A 'TUDE

Unless otherwise identified, Scripture quotations are taken from *New American Standard Bible* (NASB) © 1960, 1963, 1968, 1971, 1973, 1975, and 1977 by The Lockman Foundation. Used by permission. Also quoted: *The Amplified Bible* © 1965, Zondervan Publishing House, and the King James Version (KJV).
"Chuckles in the Cemetery" is used with permission, as is the quote from *Disciples Are Made Not Born,* © 1974 SP Publications, Inc.
"Change My Heart, O God," by Eddie Espinosa, © 1982, Mercy Publishing. All rights reserved. International copyright secured. Used by permission.

Editor: Janet Kobobel Grant
        Larry K. Weeden
Cover design: Jason Parish
Back cover photo: Nicole Owens

Printed in the United States of America

*To my
antique friend
Carol Porter,
who is full
of 'tudes—
all good!*

Contents

Acknowledgments

I offer my ongoing appreciation to my family—Les; Marty; Jason; Danya, my brand-new, beautiful, first daughter-in-law; and my spunky, 80-year-old mom, Rebecca. Les, I have loved you since we were children. That has never changed—except to grow deeper and sweeter. Marty, you were invaluable to me as my computer-rescue person. Thank you, thank you. I would have been lost in cyberspace (whatever that is) without you.

Special thanks to my secretary, Jill Scribner, who put up with my book 'tudes yea, these many months. Your warmth, charm, and assistance are a bright spot in my day. Thanks to Debbie Wirwille, who helps to keep my home in order and always takes time to respond to my stories. Lisa Harper, your incredible energy, outrageous sense of humor, and creative friendship were a gift to me during these months of toil. Jan Frank, your calls (filled with chuckles and encouragement) were often the nudge I needed to get back to my computer. How did you know? Virginia Lukei, thank you for continuing to believe in me and for me. Also, Lana Bateman and Donna Alberta, you are two zany friends who add sparkle to any day.

I would be remiss if I didn't thank the following three couples for supporting me with their friendships: Bruce and Carol Porter, Paul and Ann Meredith, and Gene and Ruthann Bell. I will always be grateful.

Janet Kobobel Grant, how I admire you. Your wit, brilliance, and insight are enhanced by your sterling character. How fortunate I am to have you in my life as my editor and friend.

Time

(tōōd′ tĭm) n.

Dictionary's definition:
A manner of carrying oneself.

Patsy's definition:
A `tude for all seasons.

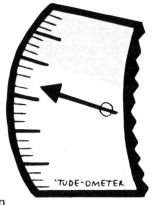

'TUDE-OMETER

Tami, who was seven, and Mindy, who was four, went to visit their grandma. After a few hours, as can sometimes happen at Grandma's house, the girls grew restless. Big sister began to notice that bored little sister was following her everywhere. In an attempt to lose her sibling shadow, Tami slipped into the bathroom and began to brush her hair—vigorously. Much to her aggravation, Mindy appeared at the bathroom door and gawked at Tami's every move.

"What are you looking at?" spewed Tami.

Insulted by her sister's lack of hospitality, Mindy crossed her arms and asked, "What's wrong with your attitude?"

Tami shook her head in disgust and with hand on hip replied, "You don't even know what an attitude is."

Insulted, lip-quivering Mindy stamped her foot and retorted, "I do, too. It's . . . it's . . . it's something that stinks!"

How true. Stinky attitudes are airborne. They waft around and add to the pollution on planet earth. But we don't have to take a deep breath to detect attitudes; they're as obvious as a new pair of iridescent sneakers. Just as surely as we wear our Liz Claibornes and Ralph Laurens, we can be seen strutting, sneaking, and slumping around in our negative 'tudes. A raised eyebrow, a leer, a sigh, a tilted head, folded arms, and pursed lips are just some of the outward adornments that give away our inner attitudes.

Nell provided her co-worker Sue with an elaborate display of attitude as they wended their way to lunch. Nell talked nonstop about her rough week. She whined and wailed over everything from escalating taxes to her boss's unfair expectations to her unending household duties. When Nell paused to take a breath, Sue, who had obviously had an ear full, shook her head and declared, "Girlfriend, you are really sportin' a 'tude!"

Yep, "sportin' a 'tude" pretty much describes my wardrobe more often than I'd like to admit. At times I've even worn the layered look, simultaneously sporting several 'tudes of questionable taste.

But I'm not alone. A group of young women who had just heard me speak on sportin' a 'tude were chatting among themselves when one of the gals confessed, "My problem is sometimes I have a 'tude on top of a 'tude."

Her friend responded, "Well, I get a 'tude, on top of a 'tude, on top of a 'tude."

The third friend quickly chirped, "Why, that sounds like a multi*tude* to me!"

The dictionary defines an attitude as "a position of the body or manner of carrying oneself, indicative of a mood or condition; a state of mind or feeling with regard to some manner; disposition."

Hmm, sounds like all we have to do to stop sportin' a 'tude is reposition our position, recondition our condition, and dispose of our disposition. Oh, my, this could take time. No, make that surgery.

When my husband, Les, had a heart bypass, I learned that during the operation, the doctor would hold Les's heart in his hand. I said to a friend, "He's going to get fingerprints on it."

Her response was, "Grow up, Patsy, the doctor will wear gloves."
What I was trying to say was that the surgeon's holding Les's
heart was so invasive, so personal, so intimate. I think that's the
scary part of looking at the condition of our attitudes as well. That
kind of examination opens us up to the heart of who we are deep
inside ourselves. I suspect that might not be a pretty sight.

The good news is that not all 'tudes have to be eliminated. Some
of them benefit us, motivate us, deepen us, and inspire others.
Embracing life-giving attitudes more fully will add to our well-
being, enhance our relationships, and clothe us in honorable attire.

Consider Daniel: He was a prayer warrior, a lion tamer, a vision-
ary, and a connoisseur of carrots. Huh? Carrots?

No kidding. As a teenager, Daniel was dragged from his home-
land and tossed into the clinker. He was then offered tantalizing
morsels from the king's menu but chose veggies instead.

That would be like a group of teens ordering ten super-duper
pizza supremes, to be washed down with your leading cola, quickly
followed by hot fudge sundaes. But one fellow in the group says,
"No, thank you. But if you have any eggplant, spinach, and beets,
I'd sure be one happy camper. Oh, yes, and if it's not too much
trouble, would you mind bringing me a big, icy tumbler of H_2O?"
Then he orders the same for his three closest buddies. His food
fetish sure would make me think twice before I palled around with
ol' dietary Dan. Not that I couldn't benefit from such nutritional
nuggets, but for me to choose peas over pepperonis—p-l-e-a-s-e—
would be highly unlikely.

Under the circumstances, who would have been shocked if this
kidnapped youngster had chosen wine over watercress? A few nips
of the king's bubbly could have temporarily eased his pain and
helped him forget about home. Besides, who would want to risk
upsetting his captors?

What enabled Daniel to show such courage as well as dietary discipline? Daniel 1:8 provides the clue: "*But Daniel made up his mind* that he would not defile himself with the king's choice food or with the wine which he drank" (italics mine).

The "but" tells us the situation was not of Daniel's choosing. Then following that scriptural beeper, we see how Daniel adjusted his attitude when he "made up his mind." The surgery of imprisonment exposed, and perhaps defined, Daniel's attitude to obey God even in life's unexpected disappointments. He was determined not to use his misfortune as an excuse to sin. Daniel didn't allow his imprisoned position to determine his condition or his disposition. The result was that he found favor, as did his buddies, in the king's eyes.

Folks, that's what it's all about, this thing called life—finding favor in the eyes of the King. For it's in the Lord's presence that we find the presence of mind to dress up in godliness and not to spend our lives sportin' stinky 'tudes.

Join me as we playfully—and purposefully—consider our attitudes and more importantly consider the only One who can surgically change our hearts.

> Change my heart, O God,
> Make it ever true,
> Change my heart, O God,
> May I be like You.

Rude 'Tude

(rōōd tōōd) n.

Dictionary's definition:
Ill-mannered.

Patsy's definition:
Snit fit.

'TUDE-OMETER

The woman was definitely out of control. Her face blazed like the noonday sun, and her purple arteries puffed and pulsated in time to her temper tantrum. She leapt repeatedly into the air and, in an ear-piercing voice, shrieked loud enough to drown out the airport P.A. system.

Our plane had been delayed not once, not twice, but four times. Then they canceled the flight. This change of plans was evidently more than hotheaded Hannah could handle. While the majority of the disgruntled passengers obediently formed a line to be rebooked on a later flight, Hannah Reeboked to the nearest phone and called the airlines.

When her call connected, her manners disconnected. She ranted so loudly that she soon gained an audience of about a hundred people. This momentary stardom seemed to add to her head of steam, for she reached over, picked up a second phone, and dialed the airline's number again, this time reaching a different clerk. Then she held the receivers in front of her and verbally let loose into both phones at the same time.

Ms. Hothead gave new definition to the phrase "talking out of both sides of your mouth at the same time." She proved that she was ambidextrous and aerobic as she jumped and juggled her phones and her phonics. She definitely had a two-fisted rude 'tude.

We seem to be a generation suffering from a "be kind to your brother" blight. Rather than "be nice," the slogan "fight, fight, fight for your rights!" rings throughout our land. Curt customers, irksome employees, belligerent bosses, testy teachers, and snarling students are frequently the norm instead of the exception.

My sweet-natured young friend Missy had a customer return an item of clothing to the dress store where Missy worked. The customer called Missy every name in the book (not the Good Book, either) because she was dissatisfied with her purchase. Imagine that we would allow an article of clothing to have greater value and higher priority than the treatment of a human soul!

Yet I, too, have been a rude 'tuder. In an intolerant moment, I have shared not from my heart but from my heat. My rudeness is often a misdirected vent for my anger. And my suppression with one person can lead to my aggression with another. I've found that to keep short accounts with the Lord and others is imperative if I am to soften my reactions to people who cause me inconveniences and disruptions.

Shakespeare penned, "Rude am I in speech, and little blessed with the soft phrase of peace." The "soft phrase of peace" catches my ear and convicts my heart. How sweet the sound of phrases of peace like "Please," "Thank you," "Excuse me," "You go first," "Let me help," and "I'm sorry."

Scripture takes us a step further than Shakespeare and tells us the results of our words. "A soft answer turns away wrath: but grievous words stir up anger" (Prov. 15:1, Amplified).

Imagine how stirred up Job's wife must have been when she lashed out and told him, "Curse God and die!" Not exactly words of comfort. Not that we couldn't understand that Mrs. Job was in emotional turmoil big time. They had just lost everyone and everything most precious to them. But the soft phrase of peace could have offered them both a moment of consolation rather than separation and isolation.

Consolation brings us together in our losses, which helps to make them more bearable. But because we're attracted to opposites, a couple will often process problems in opposite ways. That leaves the door open for additional pain, the pain of misunderstanding.

Maybe Mrs. Job became hostile when she heard her husband worshiping God after the death of their children. She may have considered Job's actions rude in light of their catastrophic losses. The Lord's allowing them to experience severe problems may have stirred her wrath.

Job's reaction was to seek the Lord in worship. Perhaps that was the only way he knew to maintain his grip on sanity. They suffered the same loss, but Mr. and Mrs. Job processed it, at least initially, differently.

Being different isn't the major divider, however. Judging another person's heart is what sparks a rude 'tude. When I decide to measure and determine the contents of your heart, I set myself up as judge. Often I'm wrong in my finite assessments, basing them on my limited experiences and my fluctuating personality. Along with my high percentage of error in evaluating someone's inner thoughts, when I judge I bring judgment on myself (see Matt. 7:1-2). When I play judge, I add heat to my own already volatile condition. That's when the sparks really begin to fly.

Ever notice how sparks fly in the New Testament every time we approach an account of the Pharisees? Talk about rude'tuders! Seems those pompous puppets of the law preferred traditions to truth, judgment to justice, and malice to manners. The Pharisees' headiness got in the way of their hearts, and they chose to embrace a lie instead of the Liberator. Again and again the Lord warned them against their rude and unrighteous behavior: "Woe to you . . ."

Woe is a word like *alas*, with a hefty helping of indictment uttered in grief and (or) indignation. For it saddens and offends God's heart when our words and our ways don't line up with His will. The Lord isn't looking for perfection in our lives, but I do believe He expects progress.

Peter the impulsive disciple had problems with things like sandals, swords, and seaweed. I'm sure he wondered if he would ever get his walk of faith right. But it was hard for him to walk when his sandal kept getting stuck to the roof of his mouth.

Speaking of sandals, within moments of stepping onto the water to walk to the Lord, Peter's sandals began to take on water, and he started to sink. Treading water in a robe is tricky, and somewhere between Peter's spitting kelp and yelling "Help!" Jesus came to his rescue.

Then there was the incident in which Peter lopped off the guard's ear. No doubt about it, Peter proved he could be presumptuous and rude. Yet the Lord saw within Peter the potential, with progress, to become a foundational man of faith.

We hear and see one of Peter's personal steps of progress when Jesus asked the disciples, "But who do you say that I am?" and Peter responded, "Thou art the Christ, the Son of the living God" (Matt. 16:15-16, KJV).

Now, that's a soft (and powerful) phrase of peace: "Thou art the Christ, the Son of the living God." If we will fully embrace this truth, it will caution us in our words and cushion our actions toward others. When we're aware of Christ's living presence in our lives, we will then have the presence of mind to draw from His reserve, that we might become peaceable people instead of contentious ones.

Remember hotheaded Hannah? How different her impact on those around her could have been had she understood Someone bigger than the airlines ultimately controls the disappointments and destinations of our lives. Hannah was not wrong to feel frustrated. Even registering a complaint could have been warranted. But she paid an inner price—her peace—when she allowed her fury to dictate her behavior. And she left others verbally whiplashed by her rudeness.

We'll need more than a refresher course from Ms. Manners to help with our behavior. If we're to be truly gentle women and gentle men, it will take a work within us by our gentle Lord Jesus.

3

Pleni-tude

(plen´ i to͞od) n.

Dictionary's definition:
Abundance.

Patsy's definition:
Lots and lots of stuff.

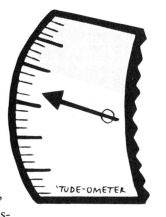

'TUDE-OMETER

I have the delightful privilege of being part of a speaking tour with three gifted women. We laugh a lot both on and off the platform, which makes the experience fun and memorable. Along with the laughter, I find I lean in to glean from their wisdom, I dab at tears of empathy, and I nod in agreement at the been-there-done-that segments.

One of those times is when Luci Swindoll talks about her "stuff." It's all I can do not to fall on the floor in a tantrum of guffaws as she explains her desire to have her own row on airplanes so she'll have enough space for her stuff. That tickles me because of my own obsession with stuff.

On a recent flight home, Les and I were in the center of a wide body (airplane, of course). The plane seemed to be designed so that each time we moved, we could puncture each other with our elbows. In this restricted space, I then had the challenge of gaining access to my stuff. And believe me, I had brought plenty of stuff. I had crosswords, magazines, snacks, manuscript, newspaper, planner, and my Bible. You can only imagine how Les on one side of me and a woman on the other loved being jabbed and disrupted by my aerobic shenanigans as I wrestled my stuff in and out of my briefcase. Call it a short attention span, but I find it difficult to go anywhere without carrying enough paraphernalia to see me through, say, a hijacking.

My house is full of stuff, too. Our home is small, but I've filled it as though it were large. I call it cozy, but there are those who would call it claustrophobic. My wall-to-wall decorating has reduced our floor space to the point that one might feel, on entering my living room, that he or she were wearing it rather than sitting in it. But one needs plenty of stuff . . . doesn't one?

What is this romance that America, the land of plenty, has with stuff, anyway? Does it make us smarter? (Duh, I don't think so.) Does it save us time? (Are you kidding? It takes up our time to maintain it.) Does it make us more popular? (Sure, to freeloaders, salespeople, and tax collectors.) Does it improve our looks? (It adds worry lines as we work to protect our stuff from "stuff" thieves; they're everywhere, you know.) There must be some reason many of us have a fetish for belongings. Do you think it fills a need? (Evidently not for long, as we scurry to the nearest stuff store to repair and replace—what else?—our stuff.)

Guess what Les and I did? We rented a storage building for our extra stuff. Imagine a monthly bill to pay for a roomful of unused stuff. Of course, one never knows when one might need a felt skirt with a pink poodle on it; a now-somewhat-oval, glow-in-the-dark hula hoop; a 1989 license plate; or a pair of (egads) chartreuse living room lamps.

One day, my neighbor Alicia placed an office chair at the curb in front of her home and put a "free" sign on it. I couldn't sprint over fast enough. A freebie—that's my idea of a quick fix for my need for stuff. I rolled that chair down the sidewalk, up our driveway, and right into my crowded office.

To make room for the office chair, we moved the couch into the garage. To make room for the couch in the garage, we moved the pinball machines into my son's apartment. To make room for the pinball machines, my son gave a dresser to some friends. To make room for the dresser . . . well, you get the idea. We'll go to great lengths to make room for our stuff.

My friends Ann and Linda own a stuff store—a classy one. Sometimes they let me play store. I help them select new stuff and arrange displays, and occasionally they even allow me to be head of the stuff and watch the store—for a couple of minutes. You can never leave a stuff person in a stuff store for long unchaperoned.

Sometimes I tire of my stuff. Then I have a stuff sale with my friend Carol. Well, actually what happens is I buy her old stuff, and she buys mine. That way we maintain our plenitude, but we somehow deceive ourselves into believing we've pared down. The added advantage is we can visit our stuff at each other's homes, sort of like joint custody. Sometimes I'll even repossess some stuff if I've really missed it.

Carol and I believe stuff people naturally gravitate to each other. We think that's because we, well, like each other's stuff. But Carol's house doesn't appear as stuffed as mine. That's because she not only has more floor space, but she also has a stuffer's dream, a two-story barn to hold her overflow, which is far better than renting a shed. You can access the barn easier, it gives you more latitude, and you don't feel as guilty because no monthly storage charge crosses your already-paper-laden desk.

Occasionally Carol and I have a stuff-arranging party. That's where we take turns telling each other different ways to display our you-know-what so that the you-know-what appears to be new. And if we're truly creative in our placement, we can even carve out space for another trunk load of stuff. (I had to say it.)

I once heard a friend say she wouldn't need another dish as long as she lived. I couldn't imagine that . . . until now. My bulging cupboards can barely hold all my dishes, and that's after I've given away three sets. And worse yet, I don't even cook. Who has time to cook? I'm too busy taking care of my . . . my . . . items.

Stuff has to be polished, buffed, waxed, stripped, sized, primed, oiled, shook, dusted, watered, washed (yawn), pressed, bleached, stretched, dyed, scrubbed, trimmed, hemmed, hung, hammered, leveled, sprayed, shampooed (z-z-z), adjusted, wired, glued, swept, painted, lacquered, and fluffed, to name just a few of our exercises (in futility). No wonder we're a weary nation; we've worn ourselves down to the nubbins preserving our _ _ _ ff.

Then, of course, there's the concern of who to leave our stuff to. Families don't always value some of our best stuff. I have an old, wooden toolbox that I treasure. I have it laden with things on my covered porch. Yes, it's worn, faded, and marred, but I think it's charming. My sons, though, on more than one occasion have announced that at my demise, they're going to use the box as (shudder) firewood. I've since decided that I would bequeath this prize to a friend who respectfully wants to fill it with some of her prime stuff. Now, that's a buddy and a more worthy use of one of my best pieces of stuff. It will comfort me, somehow, to know my stuff will be full of her stuff.

I wonder if it would be wrong to ask my loved ones to, instead of burying me—yeah, you guessed it—stuff me. (Roy Rogers did Trigger.) But instead of displaying me in a museum (neigh), they could just lean me in the corner and surround me with my stuff. (Yea!) Not that it will matter to me then, because, for the first time, I won't need, want, or require any more stuff—free at last, free at last!

4

Mood
'Tude

(mōod′ tōod) n.

Dictionary's definition:
Shifting disposition.

Patsy's definition:
Inner tantrum.

If you were to integrate the Little Rascals into one personality, you would have my six-year-old nephew, Nicholas. He has the hugability of Porky, the rascality of Butch, the determination of Spanky, the innocence of Buckwheat, the

'TUDE-OMETER

charm of Darla, and the singing ability of Alfalfa.

The latter we found out recently when my sister, Elizabeth, went to pick him up from school. Seems Elizabeth was frustrated from a hectic day, and when Nicholas had an agenda different from hers, they ended up at odds with each other. Nicholas could see his mom was in a bad mood and that he wasn't going to get his way. He then developed his own mood. After silent moments of heavy air had hung between them, he began to sing the song Alfalfa had sung to Darla in the Little Rascals movie. Alfalfa had crooned, "You are so beau-ti-ful to me." Nicholas, though, made a slight editorial adjustment. While looking out the window, as if singing to no one in particular, he trilled, "You are so pit-i-ful to me."

Mom didn't find the humor in his lyrics until later . . . much later. Then she chuckled to herself, realizing Nicholas had found the safest way he could think of to circumvent her mood and vent his.

Moods can hang between us like heavy draperies. They can separate us, isolate us, and even violate us. Moods can be signs of unresolved issues: damage, anger, depression, immaturity, grief, hormones, health, and a loss of or need for control.

As a little girl, when I pouted, it brought about desired results. So I carried that into my adult life. I used quiet hostility (often unconsciously) to manipulate people, especially my husband. Les frequently experienced the chilling effects of my emotional distance and my silent temper tantrum. Years of childish actions passed before I realized how selfish and destructive my moody behavior was. It wasn't easy to break my old response patterns, but it was liberating. I gradually learned not to give in to swings in my emotions but to give up my need to be in control. Occasionally I feel myself sinking into an old mood, but I'm more open and honest now, two responses that can help free us from unhealthy behavior.

King Ahab obviously had experienced that sinking feeling in his life. Seems the king was in a downer over dirt. He was, if you'll excuse the phrase, filthy rich. He owned plenty of land, but he wanted his neighbor Naboth's vineyard in which to plant a vegetable garden because it backed up to the king's palace. Naboth wasn't willing to give up this land for any price. It was an inheritance from his father. So what did the High Muck-a-Muck do? The pitiful potentate pouted.

Scripture tells us, "He lay down on his bed and turned away his face and ate no food" (1 Kings 21:4b). The king did some big-time boo-hooing on his bed over his broccoli's future bed until Queen Jezebel came to his rescue. She took one look at Ol' Sad Sack and asked, "How is it that your spirit is so sullen that you are not eating food?" (He was hoping she had noticed.) I can just imagine Ahab's lower lip hanging and shaking slightly when he told her, "Naboth said, 'I will not give you my vineyard.'" Sniff, sniff.

The queen's first response sounded as if she told him, "Grow a brain!" Well, actually what she said was, "Do you now reign over Israel?" In other words, "Use your power to get what you want, Bozo." (She didn't realize it, but he just had.)

Before Ahab could respond, his codependent cohort, the Queen Bee, injected her deadly venom in the form of a plot. And we're not talking garden plot; we're talking burial. She set up Naboth to be killed.

When Naboth was down and (six feet) under, Ahab "arose to go down to the vineyard of Naboth the Jezreelite, to take possession of it" (1 Kings 21:16). My, my, what a transformation occurred in the royal rascal. Once he got what he wanted, Ahab leapt out of his "grave" clothes and into his bib overalls. Seems his appetite had returned, and he was hankering for some homegrown vittles. There's something about a mood 'tude that causes a powerful appetite. (I wonder if it's all the effort it takes to work one up?)

But the king's hunger pangs ceased when the prophet Elijah announced Ahab was about to "go to the dogs" for his part in Naboth's demise. Nibbles—I mean Kibbles—and Bits takes on new meaning when it's you the dogs are nibbling and biting. The king traded in his bibs for sackcloth, humbled himself before the Lord, and asked the Lord for what Ahab hadn't given Naboth—mercy.

We seem to be quick to yell judgment toward others while crying mercy for ourselves. Isn't that right, Jonah?

Now, there was a moody guy if ever I met one. Mr. Doom & Gloom called down judgment on Nineveh and then sat ringside to watch the people perish. But when God extended the city mercy, Jonah was miffed. A megamood (about the size of a large fish) swallowed the pitiful prophet. Jonah confessed he would rather die than not have things turn out the way he wanted.

He actually complained because God was too gracious and too

compassionate. And worst of all, from Jonah's perspective, God is "one who relents concerning calamity" (Jonah 4:2).

The Lord decided to let Jonah cool his jets under the shade of an appointed plant. Some believe it was a castor oil plant. It certainly had a medicinal effect. In fact, the experience was a bitter pill for Jonah to swallow, because just about the time he was joyfully basking in the plant's shade, the worm turned. The only thing that had brought him relief and pleasure from the pressures of life was taken from him.

Isn't that how it goes for mood-tuders? They often feel picked on and plotted against. It seems to them that when life starts to take a turn for the best, they can count on some intruder to come along and eat holes in their happiness. Their favorite line is "I knew it was too good to be true." (Don't ask me how I know this.)

Jonah's joy went as deep as the roots of the plant, which overnight withered and died. Hot from the searing sun and from his scorching temper, he once again asked God to take his life. I guess Jonah forgot that God is in charge of the decision on the length of our lives; we're in charge of what we make of it. And the quality of our lives remains shallow or deep depending on what we're rooted in—our will or His.

From a little boy who couldn't get his mom to do what he wanted, to Ahab who couldn't get Naboth to do what he wanted, to Jonah who couldn't get God to do what he wanted, we begin to see a pattern. A pit-i-ful pattern of our moody struggle to be in control of the uncontrollable—life and others.

The book of Jonah closes with questions. That left me pondering. Twice the Lord asked His melancholy messenger, "Do you have good reason to be angry? Do you have good reason to be angry?"

5

Fini-tude

(fī′ ni tōōd) n.

Dictionary's definition:
Condition of being limited.

Patsy's definition:
A sizable deference.

I am limited. I can exist in this life for only a measured amount of time. As hard as I persist, a day will come when my persistence won't matter. I was designed to endure many things, but my endurance has boundaries I didn't set. I am finite.

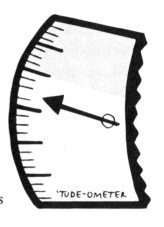

'TUDE-OMETER

The issue of our finitude is the most difficult of life's restrictions to embrace. But if we don't embrace it, we'll have no choice except to go out screaming and kicking. And isn't that the way we came in? Surely those of us who have journeyed for some years on this earth would hope we had grown enough in grace to accept our limitedness, to have made peace not only with our past, but also with our destiny. Yet I struggle at times.

A young friend, Julia, passed me in a gift store and headed for the card racks. We greeted each other, and she mentioned she was looking for an anniversary card for her husband. "How many years?" I inquired casually.

"Three," she cooed with a smile of newlywed delight.

Three? I said to myself. *Three?* The number was a jolt to my menopausal brain. Les and I have been married 33 years at the time I'm writing this. Whoa, count them—33 big ones. Where, oh where did all those years go? I'd like to kick and scream over their quick passage, but I'm too worn out.

I've noticed since turning 50 and being smack-dab in the middle of my change of life that I sometimes feel frantic, as if I'm charging to the finish line—and I'm not finished! The older I become, the more I want to do, see, and experience, and yet the days aren't long enough, nor my energy sufficient, for me to attain all my desires.

Fifty is heralded as the youth of old age, but it's also the beginning of the end of our age. What did God promise us at most in this life? Psalm 90:10 tells us, "As for the days of our life, they contain seventy years, or if due to strength, eighty years."

Let's see, that tells me that I possibly have 30 years left. That's not bad, except that unlike news flashes that bring information, my hot flashes have erased everything I've ever known or thought I knew. My brain is now the consistency of ABC gum (Already Been Chewed). That leaves me at times grappling to find two thoughts that are even distant relatives to one another, which means I'll finish out my years on a mental dimmer switch. Talk about learning to live with limits!

Not only am I a few wires short of a mental connection, but my body parts are also getting shoddy. I can no longer touch my toes. In fact, I can't even see them. Between my unfocused vision and my overblown midsection, checking out the shine on my shoes is no longer a convenient option. My increased weight and my decreased metabolism have left me heavy in the saddlebags and slowed my trot to a totter.

I wonder if all this disintegration has to do with John the Baptist's statement, "I must decrease and He must increase."

How can the infinite increase? Perhaps what John was saying was that his ministry and life would have an end, but there is One who is endless. Death puts us up close and personal with our finitude and His infinitude.

When I was growing up, whenever I acted as though I had all the answers, my southern-bred momma would remind me, "Young lady, you are getting a little too big for your britches." Little big britches—yep, that was me. I still have that problem when little ol' finite me thinks I know more than I actually do.

I think the scribes needed a momma to remind them about their bigness. *Haughty* certainly described those men of the cloth who were bound up in self-importance. They tried repeatedly to trap Jesus in word or deed, only to have their verbiage expose their own filthy hearts. They flaunted memorized portions of Scripture, trying to incriminate Jesus to the multitudes and diminish His influence. He, in turn, spoke unadulterated truth. And like a straight arrow, the truth punctured the scribes' inflated egos, sending them scurrying into dark corners to mend their big britches and plot their next vicious attack.

It's scary to think the scribes regularly handled the Scriptures and missed the point. They memorized but never internalized. Instead they became heady and haughty. Talk about not recognizing your limits! The scribes saw themselves as superior, when in truth they were spiritual slugs. They grew fat feeding on their own arrogance and vanity.

King Solomon said, "Vanity of vanities! All is vanity." Sol started out the wisest man and ended up the most disillusioned. What happened to the wise guy, anyway? Do you think being so smart caused him to get too big for his britches?

Scripture tells us to have a sane estimate of our value (see Rom. 12:3). We actually have dynamic (restricted) potential. We can be more than we realize but not so big that we can alter our certain end.

Talk about big . . . Goliath knew that the young boy David had outgrown his shepherd's britches when the youth challenged the giant bully to a free-for-all. What Goliath didn't understand was that little David came in the big strength of the Lord. The shepherd slung his sling and slew the sarcastic sap with his sack of smooth stones. Goliath, felled like an oak, never knew what hit him.

Talk about heady . . . check out David's trophy (see 1 Sam. 17:57). Goliath saw *himself* as big (too big for his mammoth trousers), whereas David saw *God* as big.

Joshua, our five-year-old great-nephew, had a mammoth trouser episode. Josh believes no task is beyond his ability. So, with his daddy's saw in hand, he made an architectural adjustment to their home. Now, why Josh decided the stair railing should be removed is beyond us. But the repeated notches and gashes in the railing did prove he had a good working grip on his equipment. He felt quite satisfied with his penetrating progress until the foreman, Joshua's mom, walked onto his work site. Later the building inspector, his dad, clearly expressed his feelings to Josh regarding his future in the construction field. Seems Joshua was forced into early retirement—at least until he was bigger.

I thought I was bigger at 12 because I could look eye to eye with my mom. When I turned 13, I soared past her four-foot-10-inch frame. Okay, okay, *soared* may be a stretch, but I did inch past her. By 15, I was a lumbering five feet tall. I thought I was so cool because I was taller than my mom. She used to tell me, "One day you'll learn that being bigger than me doesn't mean much." Sure enough, talk about discovering your limits!

The truth is we're all little (from Patsy Clairmont to Goliath), and God is big. We're small, and He's great. He's wise; at best, we're wise guys. We're finite, and He is infinite.

6

Habi-
tude

(hab´ e to͞od) n.

Dictionary's definition:
Customary behavior.

Patsy's definition:
Knee-jerk quirk.

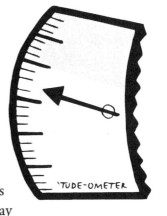

‘TUDE-OMETER

Life is habit-forming, and habits help to give life form. Without habits, we would be like scared rabbits, running hither and yon, exhausted from our efforts while not making any progress. (Hmm, sounds vaguely convicting.) That's not to say that all habits lend themselves to progress. In fact, some are downright aggravating, dumbfounding, and unproductive.

For instance, my friend Paul collects dead car batteries. That drives his wife, Ann, wacko. "Why, Paul? Just tell me why," she insisted one day.

He confessed that years ago, a person could sell defunct batteries for five dollars, and he just fell into the habit of hanging on to them. ("I've always done it this way.") Ann reached inside her purse and extracted a $20 bill, quipping, "Here, Paul. Now get rid of them."

Paul's dead batteries remind me of a habit at our home. Les always rises first in the morning, followed, in t-i-m-e, by his sputtering, half-charged wife. On that rare occasion when I speed out of bed ahead of him, it seems to drain the charge out of his battery. My appearing in a vertical position while he's still horizontal is not only shocking, but it also breaks the pattern of Les's morning. He will then linger longer than his norm between the sheets, and upon arising, he'll wander aimlessly for a while before he can get back into a routine that feels right.

We are creatures with patterns, and those patterns help us to define our direction. When someone changes the game plan, it takes time to find our rhythm again.

Speaking of rhythm, my parents were both finger thumpers. They would thump out mystery tunes on the table in time to their stress level, which increased ours as their kids. We would gladly have paid them big time to tune down or turn off their nervous music-makers.

My dad was also a change jiggler. He would shake his pants pocket of change while he talked. Maybe this habit came out of the Great Depression, when money was scarce and that left him enamored with the jingle of coins. Whatever caused him to develop the habit, it was music to my ears. I knew the sound meant I could hit him up for jukebox money. With a quarter, I could play five songs. Often I would play the same song for all five selections: "This Old House," sung by Teresa Brewer. By the third time Teresa was belting out her song, people in the restaurant seemed slightly amused. The fourth time, they would roll their eyes and glance around to try to figure out who the obsessive nitwit was. And by the fifth replay, people were downright annoyed, especially the financier, my dad.

Yep, I guess we all have habits that make others jumpy and grumpy. My son Jason and his wife, Danya, love to crunch ice. As far as I'm concerned, they might as well drag their fingernails down a chalkboard. They've learned that if they must crunch when I'm around, they should go to another floor of the house—or another house.

I, on the other hand, am a fanatical picker-upper. I have the aggravating tendency to pluck up pop glasses or coffee cups before people are finished. In fact, I move so rapidly that I have them washed and back in the cupboard before people realize their drink is missing. I don't mean to sabotage their thirst; it's, well . . . just a habit.

Some habits are obvious, like gum popping, nail biting, or hair twirling. Then there are the *other* habits. A friend confessed that when she's in conversation with someone, she writes that person's name with her tongue on the back of her teeth. (Honest, I didn't make that up!) Another gal then admitted she has a habit of writing her name over and over with her toes as though she's using a typewriter. I then 'fessed up that I make words out of the letters on people's license plates. (My habit seemed so sane next to theirs.) Of course, I didn't mention that every time I get into the shower, I burst into my rendition of "The Hawaiian Wedding Song." We who inhabit planet earth are a weird—I mean, a unique—lot.

Speaking of Lot, he allotted a lot for his lot in life. He gave up his extended family and moved his immediate family into jeopardy. Even after a hand-delivered, divine telegram warned Lot of danger, he still hesitated to make the right choice. He evidently had become comfy in his habit of making bad—no, let's make that *destructive*—choices.

After Lot was willing to compromise his daughters' virtue and had been resistant to holy shoves from heavenly messengers to escape, he finally fled sin city with his family. And they all lived happily ever after. Not! As is usually the case, indulging in indiscretions had its repercussions. Suffice it to say that Lot had salt added to his wounds.

Lot's life is an example of sin patterns begetting sin patterns. He's a reminder to us that destructive choices (like greed, ambivalence, and procrastination) can become habits as easily as knuckle cracking, lip biting, or spitting. (Yuck!)

Lot evidently didn't learn a lot. Even after he escaped disaster, he tried to drown his sorrows in booze and ended up committing acts of incest. Lot lost a lot.

What a contrast to the life of Daniel, who initially lost everything (family, home, freedom), only to eventually become the righteous ruler over many. Both men suffered loss, yet one became weak and one became wise. What made the difference? Let's take a peek back in time to see . . .

We find Daniel on his knees, living out his faith via his habit of prayer. Three times a day, he knelt before an open window to gain a view larger than his own. Three times a day, he acknowledged to himself and others the importance of the Almighty in his life. Three times a day, he opened his character to the character of God.

We hear the results of Daniel's determination to hold himself accountable before the Lord when the saps, I mean satraps, tried to find a reason to indict his behavior. "But they could find no ground of accusation or evidence of corruption, inasmuch as he was faithful, and no negligence or corruption was to be found in him" (Dan. 6:4).

Imagine having that kind of character scrutiny—and passing. Daniel's walk of faith was consistent whether times were tough (see Dan. 1:8), threatening (see Dan. 2:13), or thriving (see Dan. 6:28). Daniel was faithful to God even with his habits (see Dan. 6:10), and God was more than faithful to him (see Dan. 6:26-27).

Healthy habits (e.g., prayer life, pure thoughts, good manners) can assist us toward soulish ways by helping us draw boundaries on our behavior. Then, instead of being a loathsome Lot with a weak-kneed approach to life, we can be an esteemed Daniel, disciplined and dedicated. We can charge our batteries by changing our habitudes and thereby deepening our character and commitment.

Hebe-*tude*

(heb´ e tōōd) n.

Dictionary's definition:
Mental lethargy.

Patsy's definition:
Duh.

They (don't ask me who, but a bunch of someones) say Einstein used only 10 percent of his brain. Yikes! Where does that leave the rest of us?

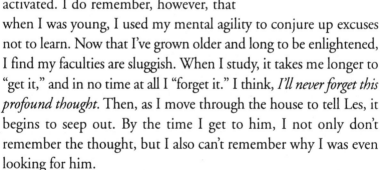

'TUDE-OMETER

I guess it means mine has not yet been activated. I do remember, however, that when I was young, I used my mental agility to conjure up excuses not to learn. Now that I've grown older and long to be enlightened, I find my faculties are sluggish. When I study, it takes me longer to "get it," and in no time at all I "forget it." I think, *I'll never forget this profound thought.* Then, as I move through the house to tell Les, it begins to seep out. By the time I get to him, I not only don't remember the thought, but I also can't remember why I was even looking for him.

Many of us regret not paying better attention when we were young, when all our brain cells were still speaking to each other. I guess we thought there was plenty of time to learn, and besides, we were pretty smart cookies. But when the cookie starts to crumble, we find life and faith are not as sweet without needed information.

For some of us, a crisis sparks our interest in further education, whether that's formal, emotional, relational, or faith education. Even though we have to work twice as hard to learn half as much as when we were young, the effort is worth it. The verse comes to mind, "My people are destroyed for lack of knowledge" (Hosea 4:6).

Of course, we also are cautioned that "knowledge makes arrogant, but love edifies" (1 Cor. 8:1b). That says to me we need to learn, but we need to do it while growing in grace. Grace allows us to serve up to others with kindness and respect what we have mentally digested.

Mental lethargy is a crime against ourselves, others, and the Lord. What we don't know can hurt us, which is probably why Peter said, "Wherefore gird up the loins of your mind" (1 Pet. 1:13, KJV). To gird up the loins of our mind means to strengthen, fortify, brace, steel, harden, and prepare our thoughts. We need to know what we believe and then believe what we know. Mental prowess is strengthened by being decisive (cut to the chase), discerning (cut to the quick), and disciplined (cut it out!).

Years ago, I saw a poster that made me giggle and groan. It read, "Some come to the fountain of knowledge to drink; I just came to gargle." I found that funny in an uncomfortable way. For I know at times that I've sloshed a valuable insight around in my head and then quickly spewed (women don't spit) it out, when what I really needed to do was swallow it.

Consider the apostle Paul, however, who swallowed volumes and knew tons of stuff. In fact, his stuffin's not only filled his head, but they also temporarily blocked his heart. It was after Paul was struck dumb that he got smart. His education took a turn from sharpening his opinions based on his faculties to deepening his understanding based on his faith. We need head smarts, but if that's all we have, we become like a forgotten book on a high shelf. Others know the volume has a lot in it, but it sits unconsulted and unread. Those who are smart and exhibit a heart, on the other hand, are approachable and desirable as companions, especially to those who long for truth.

I think Jonathan saw David as a man of wisdom and a whole lot of heart—so much so that Jonathan risked his life, his family, and his position in the kingdom to secure David's friendship. It was Jonathan's daddy, King Saul, who had the hebetude—big time. He evidently became so enamored with himself as king that he put his brain into neutral and then filled up with jealous rage. The emotion of jealousy and the action of rage must have annihilated his rational thoughts and therefore his judgment.

Saul knew the Lord had appointed him as the chosen king, yet he felt threatened by the young shepherd boy David, who honored Saul and loved God. As the king's senses dulled, his defenses were quickened. Saul didn't sharpen his wits but instead strapped on his serrated sword and came out swishing. Saul's fencing brawl ended in his own pratfall. If Saul had only used the smarts the good Lord had blessed him with, he probably would have retained his throne, aged gracefully, and had a faithful companion and successor in David. Instead, he died violently and left the latter a legacy of lunacy.

Later, when David was king, he, too, had a lull in his thinking. When his men went to war, David didn't lead them into battle, as good kings do, but instead hung out at the palace. Bored, the king went onto his porch to check out his kingdom. That's when his brain cells really went bonkers. He allowed his gray matter not to matter when he let his eyes and his hormones betray his good judgment. David and his neighbor, Bathsheba, became a little too neighborly—correction: a lot too neighborly—which resulted in duplicity, deception, and death. David had been an honorable king until he traded in his brain cells for body thrills. King David allowed Bathsheba's bath to turn into her husband's bloodshed. It's obvious the king wasn't thinking.

But we don't have to be a king or queen to be dull of mind. Or should I say "duh" of mind? Have you ever had a duh day, a day in which you should have known better about something? Like the time I backed my husband's newly purchased car over the enormous boulder at the end of my mom's driveway. It wasn't as if some boogie man had planted the rock in the driveway under cover of night. I knew the stone monument was there. I'd been in and out of her driveway hundreds of times, but, duh, I wasn't thinking. I also recall the time I sprayed on my deodorant, only to discover I had used my, duh, hair spray instead of my antiperspirant. It didn't help my perspiration problem, but it sure kept my arms in place. Then there was the time I used the can of room deodorizer for hair spray. It not only didn't hold my hair very well, but I also smelled like a pine tree for a week. Or how about the time we moved, and it took me two days to find where I had put our frozen turkey, which was now, duh, no longer frozen? When I become dull in my thinking, I get duh in my behavior.

What causes the d.t.'s (dull thinking)? Too much to do (taxes me), too little to do (spoils me), complacency (dims me), depression (numbs me), unhealthy behavior (splinters me), rebellion (indicts me), and health issues (deplete me). When we have imbalances in our behavior, it uses up our vitality, draining us of the strength to be bright. Then we pay in other areas by having duh days, which can add up to duh years, until, alas, we've led a duh life. An overused but often accurate saying is that "the light's on, but (duh) nobody's home." I'm reminded by the author of *Disciples Are Made, Not Born* that "there can be no outward shining without an inward burning."

I don't want to leave a legacy of lunacy or a heritage of hebetude. I want to will my family a history of mental clarity, competence, and compassion. For that to happen, I need to purpose to be mentally vigilant, emotionally disciplined, and spiritually attuned. Now, I'm no Einstein, but it's clear to me that I won't be able to do that on my own.

-ometer

(to͞od äm′ e ter) n.

Dictionary's definition:
Measured reactions.

Patsy's definition:
Too hot to handle.

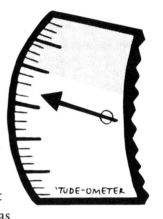

'TUDE-OMETER

If your back suddenly straightens, your neck lengthens, and you find your arms plastered squarely across your bosom, uh-oh, it could be a 'tude coming on. If your eye twitches and your hands slip past your waist to gain a death grip on your hips as you plant your feet deeper than your rosebushes, evidence is mounting. If your lips purse, your eyes fade into slits, and your forehead is drawn into a roller coaster of wrinkles . . . well, you get the idea. It's 'tude time. 'Tudes can definitely be seen.

If your pulse multiplies and your thoughts divide while your senses subtract, it all adds up. . . to an attitude. When your blood pressure percolates and your head throbs in time to the bubbles bursting in your digestive tract, it could be a you-know-what developing. 'Tudes can definitely be felt.

When I'm into a full-blown 'tude, my words fly faster than the Concorde. At times, though, I'm as silent as the eye of a hurricane with the threat of major devastation looming. When you notice my voice rising and falling more often than the president's popularity, and my s's sounding like a hissing snake, there's a good chance I'm ticked. 'Tudes can definitely be heard.

I'm aware that, on any number of occasions, I've caught a 'tude at our local grocery store—often from one of its work-worn employees. I'm also cognizant that just as often I have left one of my 'tudes with them, which they probably have passed on to the next customer. The ambushed customer then takes the 'tude into traffic, honking and harping at anyone who crosses his path. The honked-at drivers rush home and bark at their kids, who in turn do the Heimlich maneuver on the neighbor's cat. 'Tudes can definitely be shed abroad.

When 'tudes can be seen, felt, heard, and shared, you would think we would not be so easily taken captive by them. Unless we're just not in touch with ourselves. Or we've allowed too many things to stockpile inside us. Or we're feeling justified in our reactions. Out of touch, too much stuff, fuss, fuss, fuss.

That reminds me of the time I was out east, in the mountains. I had just finished speaking at a ladies' event, and a young woman was waiting in the wings to take me to the airport. My schedule had been especially demanding that season, and I found myself crisscrossing the country to try to fulfill my crammed calendar.

The driver whisked me into her pickup truck and made two unforgettable statements. Statement #1: She had 30 minutes to get me to an airport that was 50 minutes away. But (statement #2) I shouldn't be concerned because she had once been an ambulance driver. With that information, she plunged the accelerator through the floorboard and sped down the mountain. We passed several logging trucks (one on a curve), not to mention assorted other vehicles. We careened precariously close to the unfenced edges (giving me glimpses into glory). We dropped in elevation so rapidly that my eyebrows became permanently arched. I'm not certain I breathed until our tires were on level ground.

When we arrived at the airport (in the nick of time), we ran, bags in hand, to the gate. I was then rushed outside to board a microscopic airplane. How small was it? It was slightly larger than a model plane and definitely smaller than a real one. It held only a couple of passengers, including lucky, white-knuckled, nauseated me.

I hid behind my briefcase, fussing and fuming during the flight. Finally I asked myself, *How did I ever end up ridge-running with Wile E. Coyote's sister, much less find myself booked on a plane-ette that is flailing about in the jet stream?*

The answer was all too obvious. I hadn't faced my physical and personality limitations. I had taken on more than I could handle sanely, sensibly, and sweetly. Then, when it got to be too much for me, I wanted to blame others for the unwanted challenges I was facing. I was sportin' a `tude because I hadn't stopped long enough to check my `tude-ometer.

If we would listen to our body's responses, our mind's conversations, and our verbal intonations, we could begin to nip destructive attitudes in the bud. Of course, it takes more than just spotting them to overcome them. To give up an attitude takes a commitment to change, ownership of our behavior, a willingness to die to self, and a reliance on the Lord to do for us what we can't do for ourselves.

Change can be a threat, a relief, a necessity, an inconvenience, and (usually) a laborious process. Many times, personal pain has been the motivation I've needed to make critical changes in my life. When my life-temperature rises high enough, I find I'm more willing to do whatever it takes to be well again. There's nothing worse than withering in feverish agony emotionally, relationally, or spiritually. But I've also noticed that after I've made important attitudinal adjustments, the mercury begins to fall as my fever breaks, and I'm restored to good (mental, social, and spiritual) health. In other words, change is worth the effort and the cost.

I live in a delightful town with a personality problem—not

enough parking. Unfortunately, this deficiency doesn't improve my personality. Recently, after circling the parking lot in town several times, I spotted a car leaving. I picked up speed and raced around to position my vehicle to take its slot when, lo and behold, another car approached from another entrance and pulled toward the space before I could get there. The driver didn't know I had already circled the lot more times than Joshua did Jericho. But she got the idea when I sped around the corner honking like a flock of Canadian geese. She stopped her car, checked her mirror, and then politely drove away. I then zoomed into *my* spot and screeched to a halt, bumping the curb.

My friend Jill, who had witnessed my noisy maneuvering from the passenger seat of my car, looked at me in surprise and said, "I am so embarrassed." Then she speculated, "What if she knows you? What if she has read your books?"

Startled by my own behavior and sobered by the thought that I had allowed my poor attitude to turn into bad manners, I got out of the car and looked for the woman. She had just found a vacated space and was pulling her car into it. I headed in her direction. I knew I needed to apologize. I prayed she wouldn't know me; anonymity would make this confession less painful. When she slipped out of the car and turned toward me, however, I realized I *did* know her. And yes, she had read my books. My overdone aggression had turned into humble pie, and now that I was recognized, I found it even more difficult to swallow my failure.

I could have saved myself (and Jill) an embarrassing episode, and the gracious woman a jolting experience, if I had checked my `tude-ometer instead of my speedometer. In fact, let's do that now. Let's see if we're reasonable people or if it's time to change because we're attitudinally too hot to handle.

Are you often aware of having a larger response to a situation than it calls for—for example, screaming at someone for an innocent mistake, passing severe judgments against others, or outbursts that surprise even you (honk, honk)?

Do you frequently feel deficient? defective? defensive?

Do you often feel misunderstood?

Is self-pity a regular party you throw for yourself?

Do you wish you were someone else—somewhere else?

Do you overwhelm others? Are you often overwhelmed by others? by life?

Do you talk too much? too little? too loud?

Are you often uptight and in a fight-or-flight mode?

If we find ourselves identifying with more of these questions than we would like, we need to look under our attitude to the hole in our heart. If we'll take truth as far as we can on our own behalf, the Lord will begin to heal the places we can't reach, and He will expose the sin we haven't faced. That will then give us the opportunity to experience growth at a deep, life-changing level. Remember, if your 'tude-ometer's needle is stuck on the hot side, park yourself in His presence until you cool down and wise up. Take it from a former Indy 500 wannabe.

9

Exacti-*tude*

(ig zak′ te tōōd) n.

Dictionary's definition:
Being exact.

Patsy's definition:
Picky, picky, picky.

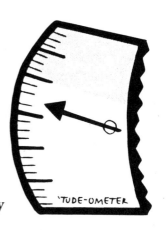

'TUDE-OMETER

My delightful neighbor Alicia alphabetizes her spices. My friend Jill is filing all her recipes in the computer. An acquaintance, Linda, dates her groceries before she puts them away. These girls have been bitten by the exactitude. But they're not alone.

For years, my mom has crocheted the most exquisite floor-length tablecloths. If she finds she missed a stitch 22 rows back, she'll rip out all the perfect rows to correct the one imperfection that no one in the world would have noticed. It hurts to watch her unravel row after row of her beautiful work in search of a mistake. But she's into exactitude. And when she completes her work, it's lovely . . . and exact.

When I was growing up, we would go on vacation every summer, usually to my parents' home state of Kentucky. My mom would start to pack days before the trip, and by the time we left, we could have entered our suitcases in a *Good Housekeeping* contest—and won. They were truly works of art. Mom would iron every item before packing and then carefully fold it and secure the corners with straight pins. Once the clothing was pinned, she would smooth it one last time with the iron. All my pj's were on the right side of the suitcase, and my pedal pushers were on the left, pinned to their matching tops. My dresses were hung and wrapped in sheets and then carefully stretched across the top of the suitcases in the trunk.

I admire people who are exacting—evidently not enough to follow in their footsteps, though, at least not in packing. If I can close my suitcase once it's packed, I consider that a worthy accomplishment. I have still more problems when I repack for my trip home. Even if I haven't purchased anything additional, once I wear my clothes, they gain weight. Those fat things refuse to fit back in the suitcase, leaving my luggage obese and overwhelmed from carrying such a hefty load.

My nightmare is that one day, what I once witnessed at the Detroit Metro Airport will happen to me. Les and I were waiting for my cases and had been almost lulled to sleep by the monotonous circling of luggage on the conveyor belt. A woman who had obviously not ironed or pinned her clothing before packing and must have been on the return segment of her trip had overtaxed her suitcase. Dangling big-time from her partially opened, circling luggage were her huge Hanes (and we're not talking socks). Her husband spotted the case, saw her unmentionables exposed and fluttering at half-mast, and had the audacity to mention them. The brute picked up the suitcase in one hand and her bloomers in the other. Holding them in the air like a sail on a schooner, he walked through the crowd, chirping, "Are these yours, Honey?"

I was mad at Les all the way home. Poor guy, of course he had nothing to do with that woman's embarrassing fiasco, but he was the only one around for me to be upset with. Besides, I wanted him to understand exactly what I would do to him if he ever embarrassed me like that.

So I guess I can be exacting on things like threats, opinions, and knickknacks. Knickknacks? Yep! I'm fanatical about the arrangement of my pretties around the house. When my friend Debbie helps me clean, I drive her crazy as I shadow her around the premises, resituating items after she dusts them.

Being an exacting person has its benefits and its detriments. For instance, I want my surgeon, my dentist, and my accountant to sport an exactitude. That's beneficial for everyone concerned. But when I nitpick about incidentals like the placement of a teacup and whether the handle should be turned to the right instead of the left, that can become detrimental. Nitpicky people are seldom sought after as good company.

I guess, though, that we all have some areas of our lives in which we're more exacting than others. What are yours?

I love a well-made bed. I don't like the sheets to be lopsided or lumpy but smoothed out and tucked tightly. I like my bed full of fluffed pillows in varying sizes, and I like the spread draped evenly. But I've learned that if I don't have time to do it exactly the way I like it, that's okay. Time won't stop, the stock market won't crash, and a bed cop won't suddenly appear and write me up for loose bedding.

My friend Lana learned some lessons about exactitude when her son's girlfriend invited her over for a birthday dinner. It turns out this gal was a gourmet cook, and Lana said it was one of the best meals she had ever eaten. Everything had been prepared exactly as it should have been.

Lana's only disappointment was that some of her good friends didn't get to sample this excellent fare. She felt her words fell short of describing something that only experience could define.

So Lana was elated when a second invitation arrived to attend an open house and to bring guests of her choice—exactly what Lana had hoped for, gourmet goodies and all. Lana regaled her friends about this dream-come-true cook.

When they arrived, Lana and her now-excited friends gathered in the living room and selected cozy seats around a tray of lovely appetizers. Eager to try them, Lana's guest Beverly selected an item and dipped it into the candle-heated sauce. She took a bite, chewed, swallowed, and then began to spit. She tried to dispose of the rest of her gourmet treat into her napkin while shaking her head in disgust.

Lana was aghast. "What's wrong?" she whispered to her friend.

"It's terrible," Beverly choked out quietly.

"Don't be silly," Lana replied, beginning to feel defensive. Then Lana, to prove her friend wrong, picked up the identical item, dipped it into the sauce, and popped it into her mouth. Her eyes began to grow larger, and she looked for a place to get rid of the disgusting stuff in her burning mouth. Her now-experienced friend handed her some napkins. Lana was confused, embarrassed, and nauseated.

She decided the offending culprit was something in the raspberry sauce. When one of the kitchen helpers walked through the room, Lana meekly asked about the sauce's contents.

"Sauce?" said the woman. "Why, that's liquid potpourri!"

Later, Lana had to admit the evening had not gone exactly as she had thought it would. The good news was that Lana and Beverly had the sweetest breath for weeks afterward.

Isn't that just like life? Seldom does it go exactly as we anticipate.

When my husband's niece Carmen had an operation as a young girl, we became concerned because she was in surgery much longer than the doctor had predicted. When the surgeons emerged, they were shaking their heads in amazement. Carmen had a lot of extra parts, they said, and they had needed to figure out exactly how she was knit together before they could accomplish their task. The operation was a success, but the doctors were still scratching their heads at her puzzling design as we left the hospital.

There is One, however, who isn't surprised by our inner workings. He understands exactly how we're put together, every stitch, for He was there when we were formed. He isn't surprised by the unexpected happenings in our lives, either, for He knew exactly what would occur. He knows even our nitpicky ways and loves us exactly the way we are. He is "the Father of lights, with whom there is no variation, or shifting shadow" (James 1:17). How grateful I am that in this fluctuating, unsure, compulsive world, a Point of Reference holds steady! Jesus is the perfect exactitude example, for He is exactly the same yesterday, today, and forever.

10

Forti-
tude

(fôr´ te tōōd) n.

Dictionary's definition:
Strength of mind.

Patsy's definition:
Heads up.

In *The Family Book of Christian Values*, Stuart and Jill Briscoe quote a poem titled "Courage." The last two lines read, "Courage is fear that has said its prayers." Those words say to me that courage doesn't always start off strong, but it can find the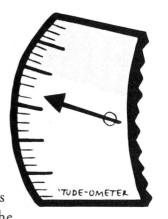

needed strength in spite of weakness—even in the midst of it. That means little knee-knocking me can qualify as potentially courageous.

I used to believe I had to feel brave before I could take steps in a scary direction. I have since learned bravery is not what you feel but what you make up your mind to do. The challenge is to "set [our] face like flint" (Isa. 50:7) in the right direction, then take the first steps onto an unsure and sometimes intimidating path, with the willingness to see it through. The result? Voila! Fortitude.

Fortitude is like buying a lifetime membership to an exercise club and then actually showing up for each session. Whoa, think about it: This isn't a word, it's an aerobics course! What an exhausting thought, a lifetime of courage! Admirable, enviable, yet it seems unattainable.

Remember Daniel in the pen, though, accused unfairly by the

men and then thrown into the den (not to be confused with the study). He never gave up (his faith), he never gave in (to their demands), he never gave over (to their ways), but he walked through each difficulty one courageous step at a time.

Or consider a more reluctant fortitude candidate: edgy Esther. Talk about having to walk a knee-knocking line—between royalty and relatives, Esther's queenly position was precarious at best. A pretty maiden, she was chosen as queen following a beauty pageant of sorts. But unbeknownst to the king, Esther came incognito. She had conveniently withheld her Jewish origin so as to avoid unnecessary pressure and to respect her uncle's counsel.

Then an enemy in the kingdom, Haman, devised a treacherous scheme to eradicate the Jews, thus threatening Esther's and her people's lives. She was alerted to the rascal's plot, thereby placing the future of her people in her trembling hands. Esther reluctantly, after big-time nudges from her honorable uncle, proceeded with a daring dinner. Between drinks and dessert, Esther served hard-boiled Haman to the king. The king gratefully couldn't digest this sneaky snake in the grass but had Haman hung out to dry. (See Esther 7.)

Esther didn't find it easy to put her life (she was young and beautiful) and lifestyle (cushy, spa city) in jeopardy for her people, especially since the last queen was banished forever for her unwillingness to be at King Ahasuerus's beck and call. Young Queen Esther was hesitant to do anything that might vex his highness. But Esther pushed past her feelings of fear and intimidation and became a female of fortitude. She spoke the truth, spared her people, and exposed a sinister plot.

Then there's the apostle Paul, a man of sagacity and tenacity. After his conversion, however, he didn't see himself that way, which was probably a key to his ongoing courage. Paul faced shipwrecks, floggings, stoning, and imprisonment with strength and, of all things, joy.

Excuse me, but if I have to wait more than a few minutes in the checkout line at the store, I'm offended and think I'm really suffering for Jesus. I don't mean to be flippant, but honestly, we in the western world seem to see simple inconveniences as indignations and hardships as unfair atrocities. Paul, on the other hand, saw danger as an opportunity to trust the Lord and hardship as a way to identify with the Savior. What a 'tude! I sure hope courageous is contagious.

Actually, instead of waiting to perchance "catch" fortitude, we can prepare ourselves for the times when we'll need strength beyond our own and courage to replace our fear. On close examination, we see the fortitude tactics implemented in the lives of Daniel, Esther, and Paul.

Repeatedly, Daniel presented himself to the Lord. Repeatedly, he made his requests known and then leaned in to listen to God, who hears our words and sees our heart. Repeatedly, amidst the demands of his influential position and threats to his life, Daniel stopped his activities to acknowledge and worship God.

No wonder enemies couldn't intimidate this mighty man of faith. No wonder lions slept peacefully in his presence. No wonder the king rejoiced at the miraculous deliverance of his esteemed counselor, Daniel the lion-hearted.

A willingness to repeatedly bend our knee to the Lord prepares us to rise up clothed in His dignity and strength. Daniel had learned through his life of exile to talk to God. Daniel had years of prayer practice by the time he faced the lions.

But Esther was a different story. She was young and inexperienced in life-threatening dilemmas. She appears to have been a cautious woman, an easy-does-it lady, a let's-not-make-any-waves kind of gal. Along came her uncle and asked her to risk her throne and possibly her life by being a bearer of bad tidings. The king had already eliminated one lippy queen, and Esther didn't want to further rile his royalty. But knowing she must do what she must do, Esther asked that her people fast, as would she and her maidens, before she chatted with his hasty highness.

What a wise young woman to entreat her extended family of faith to fast, because witnesses in humble agreement before the Lord are a powerful force. Esther feared that if she proceeded and exposed the enemy to the king, she would perish. Instead, she prospered even more than before. Now Esther was secure not only in her position with the king, but also in her position with the King of kings.

The apostle Paul knew the importance of both prayer and fasting, and he added a third cord to our rope of hope that will pull us out of our fear and into courage—Scripture.

In 2 Timothy, Paul wrote to his beloved son in the Lord and reminded him of the importance of the Word of God. It seems that those surrounding Paul had grown weary of prisons, punishments, and ongoing persecution, so they deserted him. Paul reminded Timothy that difficult times (and people) would come into his life, and he must stand firm and be courageous (whether others were or not). To prepare him for hardships, Papa Paul told Timothy to remain faithful to the Sacred Writings, for they would profit him, reprove him, correct him, and train him.

God breathed the Scriptures knowing we would need guidelines, encouragement, enlightenment, comfort, and courage.

When I read that Daniel faced lions, it strengthens me to face the growling beasts in my life. There was the time, for instance, when I was commissioned by my husband to pick up auto parts on his behalf. When I arrived at the store, I felt like a china cup in a bull ring. But I assured myself I'd be all right. All I had to do was give Les's name, and they would hand me his order.

I wonder why I live under the delusion that life is going to be simple?

The man behind the desk began to bark questions at me about the order. I think my blank stare reminded him of his mother-in-law, whom he obviously didn't care for. He began to speak louder. Yelling at me doesn't make me smarter. . . or him, either. I thought about yelling back, but he wasn't who I wanted to be like. Instead, calmly (a rare moment) and quietly (a semiprecious moment), I left. After I got home, I was so glad I hadn't joined the man in his growling behavior. It was one of those times when I faced a lion and didn't flinch or give up my personal dignity. Thanks, Daniel.

Then when I see Esther tiptoeing toward truth, I'm encouraged to continue my walk, even if, at times, I'm only taking baby steps. I'm amazed and sometimes discouraged to realize I'm still asking the Lord to help me in some of the same areas where I was asking for help years ago . . . like discipline. I still don't eat as well as I should, and my desktop looks like the leftovers from a ticker tape parade. I also tend to slump while sitting at the table. There's something so tacky about a woman who rests her chin on her plate.

Yet I have finally reduced and organized my purse. I no longer strap a trunk over my shoulder, and the contents no longer become dangerous projectiles hurling in all directions when my treasure chest is opened. I now have a petite pouch with just the necessities tucked neatly inside. Mind you, it wouldn't see me through a stint on a deserted island, as my former one could have, but my condensed system is simpler and therefore saner (not to mention lighter).

Also, even though I'm not jostling my cellulite at a gym, I did move my closet upstairs, forcing myself to climb up and down the steps many times a day. My thighs are still flapping in the breeze, but I can now reach the top step without turning greenish blue.

As for my eating habits, I'm far better informed, and I now purpose to read fat and sugar contents before purchasing. I've learned how to make my own vegetable juices, and sometimes I even drink them. I give up dessert more often than I accept it, with the exception of pumpkin pie. (I've been known to consume an entire pie without assistance.)

So, like Esther, I may not be racing to the finish line, but I am headed in the right direction. And given enough time, I may even learn how to sit up straight. Thanks, Queen Esther, for making the right choices . . . eventually.

Now when I follow Paul's journeys and jog in and out of prison with him as I read the epistles, I'm prompted to be courageous and to endure faithfully to the end. Some of the scariest steps I took in my prison (agoraphobia) days were down the steps outside my front door. I mentally held onto my rope of hope as I tentatively inched my way toward freedom. I had prayed, and I had sought the prayers of others. I did some fasting, and I was gradually becoming a student of the Scriptures. Yet even with my rope of hope, my freedom wasn't easy or fast, but it was definite and sure. I sometimes felt as if I were emotionally dangling off the edge of a cliff, but I found the rope held. In time, I regained my footing and then scrambled my way up onto a ledge. What a relief! But I knew it was just a matter of time before I would have to take another step out of my safety zone if I was ever to be well mentally, emotionally, relationally, and spiritually.

One of my first excursions out of my agoraphobia was to attend a Bible study for nervous folks. My concern was that it might be more like a babble study if the others were in as bad a shape as myself. Gratefully, the gals attending were better acquainted with the Scriptures than I was, and they were helpful in directing me to verses that encouraged me to be courageous. One of the gals introduced me to 2 Timothy 1:7: "For God hath not given us the spirit of fear; but of power, and of love, and of a sound mind" (KJV).

After years of being housebound, I learned to face my fears, trust the Lord, and experience His power, love, and a sound mind. I learned to drive a car again and to ride with others. (Today I travel extensively and continually.) Once I made it to the car, I began to attend church, and eventually I even risked sitting in the front row. Then one day, I found myself as the speaker on the platform. Wow, that's some rope!

Lost hope? There is a rope (prayer, fasting, and the Scriptures), and "a cord of three strands is not quickly torn apart" (Eccles. 4:12b). Remember, we're not born with fortitude, but we can develop into courageous people. And it also helps me to remember Who holds the other end of our rope—the One who will never let go.

Senecti-tude

(si nek´ te tōōd) n.

Dictionary's definition:
Old age.

Patsy's definition:
What, like 50 or something?

My 80-year-old mother is a kick. Mom loves to dress up every day and go somewhere. She doesn't care where as long as she can be out and about. Les and I took her out for her birthday dinner just recently. When the young waiter came to lead us to a

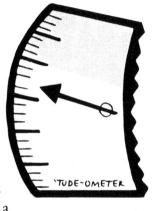

'TUDE-OMETER

table, she pointed her tiny finger at him and said in her biggest voice, "Give me the best table in the house; I'm 80."

Mom has gone through a number of health challenges: a dramatic loss of hearing, breast cancer, glaucoma, cataracts, a fractured hip, and the most frustrating of all, Parkinson's. Yet even with the fading of available information, she continues to have a delightful, if at times disconcerting, sense of humor. Mom called one day and asked me to take her to the doctor. When we arrived, the office was full of waiting patients. We sat down in chairs that were linked to the chairs next to them, putting us elbow to elbow with those on each side. As is usually the case in a waiting room, the only sounds were an occasional wheeze and the ripple of magazine pages being turned. We were all aware that even if we whispered, because of the tight proximity, everyone would be privy to our conversation.

I was innocently skimming through a *Time* magazine when my mom decided it was her time to make an announcement. As clear as a clapper striking a bell, she proclaimed, "Yep, guess I'm going to grow a mustache."

To say I was taken aback would be mild since it had never occurred to me that Mom was even considering such an undertaking. Not knowing for sure what to do with this now-public information, and feeling an obligation to respond, I asked weakly, "And why is that?"

In her inimitable way, she declared, "Because yours is getting so much longer than mine!"

Senectitude must mean the freedom to say whatever comes to your mind. Yikes! Sounds as if this latter season of our lives could be the most revealing. I think Mom is getting back at me for every labor pain she endured at my birth. The good news is that I, in my senectitude, can do the same to my children.

At a retreat I attended, I met a lovely older woman who had never married. In a conversation we had regarding funerals, she told me all her pallbearers were going to be women.

"Really?" I replied, surprised and fascinated.

"Yes," she said. "Since the men didn't want to take me out when I was living, I'm not going to let them take me out when I'm dead."

She made me giggle, as did this senectitude poem about grandmothers:

In the dim and distant past when life's tempo wasn't fast,
Grandma used to rock and knit, crochet, tat, and baby-sit.
When the kids were in a jam, they could always count on Gram,
In an age of gracious living, Grandma was the gal for giving.
Grandma now is at the gym exercising to keep slim,
She's off touring with the bunch, taking clients out to lunch,

Driving north to ski or curl, all her days are in a whirl,
Nothing seems to stop or block her now that Grandma's off
her rocker!

My mother did recognize in a public way this truth: I'm getting
older. Not only am I "off my rocker," but I've also noticed my physical resilience is becoming sluggish. Still, I was surprised last week
when even my muscles went awry. I was on a drug run (we had left
my husband's medicines in the trunk of a woman's departing vehicle), and as I sprinted (okay, okay, sauntered rapidly) to catch her,
it seemed someone threw a hardball into the back of my leg. Later,
I found out that the gripping wad in my calf was ripped muscles.

A compassionate athletic therapist came to my aid and packed
my leg in ice. He was attentive, helpful, and young. He proceeded
to tell me that "at your age," I shouldn't rub my leg in case of blood
clots. As beneficial as that insight was, actually, at my age, I don't
want anyone to bring up my age. If you know I'm old and I know
I'm old, isn't it kind of redundant? Instead of "at your age," I
would have liked him to say, "Winter's winds have weakened your
willows, and the sap's lodged in your limbs." There now, doesn't
that sound better?

I find the aging process full of surprises. Oh, I don't mean just
the negative physical changes, but the positive emotional and relational liberation as well. I've become wiser in my responses and
therefore don't feel the same unhealthy obligations to individuals I
once did. I've learned that I'm not responsible for the happiness of
others (hallelujah!), although I always want to be a giver, a
nurturer, and a true friend.

That description reminds me of Edith Gelaude and Eleanor
Barzler, two seasoned pros who give me courage to keep on keeping
on. They are amazing women full of joy and zeal. Their individual

trees have stood through a myriad of seasons. They've gone through great losses and have braved them with humor and heart. And they both continue to stretch out their fruitful branches to offer others sustenance and comfort.

Isn't that what enhances life, our willingness to invest wisely in others and to continue to be productive? Consider Elizabeth, the mother of John the Baptist. She had the surprising opportunity to bear fruit in her old age. No, I'm not speaking of when she gave birth to John but of her visitation from Mary.

Mary ran to Elizabeth for comfort and direction, and Elizabeth received her with humility and honor. Then Elizabeth opened her arms and her home to Mary for three months. *Months?* Yes, months. Two pregnant women in one house—that's a lot of hormones.

I am taken aback not only by the generous length of Mary's stay, but also by Elizabeth's greeting of homage. The aging Elizabeth showed the young maiden deference. Now, that's admirable. Elizabeth could have felt resentment that she wasn't chosen to bear the Christ child. She could have been judgmental toward Mary since she wasn't married. Elizabeth could have felt a spirit of rivalry between herself and Mary and between their firstborn sons. Instead, Elizabeth was joyous and used by God to affirm Mary's womanhood and the fruit of her womb.

Then there's 84-year-old Anna, widowed prophetess who served faithfully in the temple, awaiting the coming of the Lord. And when He came, she recognized Him, even as a mere babe in arms.

I just did a retreat in Florida. I was excited about going, because that meant I would have the added benefit of seeing my sister, Elizabeth, and her family. But we hadn't arranged a time when we would get together. So when Elizabeth came up at the end of my first talk, I didn't recognize her. She looked like herself, but I was caught up in the activity of the moment and didn't focus, even though I was looking right at her. When Elizabeth began to talk to me, her voice clicked my brain into gear, and I, embarrassed, jumped up to greet her. My one and only sister—and I didn't recognize her!

Anna, on the other hand, not only anticipated the Lord's arrival (she served night and day, fasting and praying), but she also hadn't allowed her long wait for Him to dishearten or distract her. When the Lord was finally brought to the temple, Anna instantly recognized Him and heralded His arrival. Her 84-year-old physical light may have been dimming, but Anna's mind and heart were full of the light of redemption. Anna, unlike me, wasn't embarrassed; she was emancipated. Her Redeemer had come.

When I grow up, I want to be like my mom, Edith, and Eleanor. Despite difficulties, dark days, and diseases, they carry on with verve.

When I grow up, I want to be like Elizabeth and Anna, tenderhearted toward others and sensitive to the presence of the Lord. Those are 'tudes I would sport proudly.

12

Beati-tude

(bē at´ e tōōd) n.

Dictionary's definition:
Blessed truth.

Patsy's definition:
Insight for living.

"Blessed are those who mourn, for they shall be comforted."

My friend Sheila Hamman teaches at an elementary school. One day, she gave her third-grade students an assignment to compose a letter to someone in history.

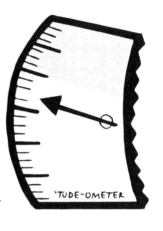

'TUDE-OMETER

One young boy decided to write to Joan of Arc. He wrote, "Joan, I'm sorry you had to go through so many bad things, but I'm glad your husband was able to get all the animals to safety."

Even though this young student had his stories crossed, I'd still give him an A+ for searching out a redeeming factor in the midst of tragedy. Children have a way of reminding us of what's really important.

Joshua, Les's nephew's son, certainly has done that for us. Joshua and his mom and dad, Mike and Michelle, live 600 miles away. We became instantly and intimately acquainted when a family crisis arose. Joshua, at age three, had to be airlifted to a hospital near our home when he was diagnosed with leukemia. He required regular treatments at the clinic in Ann Arbor. Because we were close to the hospital, Mike, Michelle, and Joshua stayed in our home before and during treatments over a two-and-a-half-year period. This allowed us the privilege of getting to know our geographically distant kin.

Joshua is his own little man. He's feisty and fidgety, and I'm almost sure he's full of rocket fuel. Joshua keeps us all on our toes.

At one point in his treatments, he received heavy doses of chemotherapy, causing him to lose his thick, red hair. We adults were sad but thought it a small price to pay if it meant Joshua would eventually be well. But Josh was devastated by his new, slick image. He couldn't comprehend, at three and a half, our concern about his future welfare; he was concerned with right now. Josh had a wardrobe of nifty hats, but they didn't make up for his lost hair. He was in mourning.

When Christmas came around, he announced to his mom that he wanted Santa to bring him hair. As a family, we would have bought Joshua anything he requested, but hair was outside our jurisdiction. We made suggestions of other gifts that would be great fun, but try as we might, we couldn't budge his decision. Michelle considered cutting her hair and weaving it into a "do" for him, although she knew a wig wouldn't satisfy her little guy's heart, much less fit his head.

As Christmas arrived, we all hoped the excitement of gift giving and receiving would distract Josh and keep him from feeling devastated when he didn't get his hair. At the first break of light, Joshua came bounding down the steps. As he circled the tree, Michelle noticed he had already been into something and had gotten dirty. She went into the kitchen, dampened a washcloth, and proceeded to wash off Joshua's dirty head. Then Michelle noticed it wasn't washing off . . . and it wasn't dirt . . . but a soft down of new hair.

After the initial excitement over his hair had settled down, Josh set about unwrapping his gifts. When he opened the last one, he once again remembered his best gift of all. He ran his hand across his head, and his eyes grew large with fresh realization. "Mom," he whispered in awe, "I have hair."

Talk about rejoicing! All other gifts paled. One of Joshua's aunts, examining his soft wisps of hair, exclaimed, "Wow! Makes me want to believe in Santa."

But Joshua's Grandma Diane wisely added, "It's somebody bigger than Santa."

Later, as they recounted the story to me, I said, "Yes, it's Someone who hears the prayers of a child."

Les and I went to visit Joshua at his northern Michigan home. His hair had grown in and was more beautiful than before. After we had been there for a while, Josh suddenly disappeared and then returned carrying a comb. He presented it to me, as a knight might his sword, so I could have the joy of combing through his lovely, bronze hair.

Joshua is under the constant threat of losing his hair again, because his treatments continue. But I don't think it will be as difficult next time, even for Josh. His miracle hair on Christmas served as a reminder to us that there is One who cares for and comforts a hurting child in ways we never could . . . and understanding that comforts us, his mourning family.

"Blessed are the peacemakers, for they shall be called sons of God."

When we decided to name our second son Jason, I didn't realize his name meant "peacemaker." Nor could I have realized how accurate that description would be. My grandmother told me you get babies through the Sears catalog, and I've wondered sometimes if that's where we acquired Jason. Then I remember my labor pains and that we look so much alike, and I realize Sears had nothing to do with this transaction. But in our family, Les, Marty, and I are far more feisty than Jason.

When he was in elementary school, the teachers would tell me that if they had a hot spot in the room, where students just couldn't get along, they would move Jason in the middle of it, and soon the squabbles would stop.

My friend Lana tells me that's because Jason is a phlegmatic personality, and phlegmatics are natural peacemakers. In fact, she says they're the human tranquilizers of society. Just having someone of that temperament enter a room can change an intense climate to a more hospitable one. Perhaps we should take a few notes on what these peacemaking personalities do, that we might become less volatile and more peaceable.

When Jason was in middle school, I wanted to teach him the importance of forgiveness. (Middle-school days seem to be such a hormonally and attitudinally disruptive period.) I asked him to think of someone he didn't like. Jason thought and thought and finally said he couldn't think of anyone. I found that amazing. Well, actually, I found that ridiculous. I could think of *tons* of people I wasn't terribly fond of; surely he could come up with *one*. Finally, in frustration I said, "Okay, okay, then think of someone who doesn't like you." Again Jason couldn't come up with a name. (My own list, for myself, was lengthy.) Now, how was I to teach this boy how to forgive when he didn't have hostile conflicts with others?

In Jason's senior year of high school, he took a trip to Florida and brought back a wardrobe of new T-shirts. He was proud, sportin' his collection of "awesome finds." Then one day he called me into his room and asked if I had washed his T-shirts. I told him I hadn't had time. So he pulled a basketful of his new shirts from the closet to show me that someone had washed them with a pair of bright pink shorts. The shorts had run all over every shirt. He asked if I thought the blotches would come out, and I said I didn't think so.

They appeared to be ruined.

I snapped up one of the shirts to go find out who the culprit was, but Jason stopped me. "Don't say anything, Mom," he protested.

Confused, I replied, "Why not?"

"You might hurt their feelings," he said.

Maybe I did get him from Sears. Honestly, if someone had just ruined my new clothes, I would want to hurt the person's feelings, at least a little. Know what I mean? Jason, though, valued his family's feelings over the cost of the shirts, and he felt the incident should be overlooked.

His brother, Marty, came along and discovered the gaudy, pink pile of stained shirts. He quietly disappeared downstairs with the basket tucked under his arm. Some time later, he reappeared carrying Jason's restored shirts. Marty had treated, soaked, washed, and dried the T-shirts. They looked spanking new. Hmm, if I remember correctly, I believe we ordered Marty from Spiegels.

I wonder if peacemakers are called the sons of God because peace is more important to them than their pride?

"Blessed are those who hunger and thirst for righteousness, for they shall be satisfied."

As a young, newly expectant mother, I experienced a rush of hormones and emotions that kept my inexperienced husband guessing what my next outrageous request might be. I had heard of cravings and even had some strong longings for certain foods at times, but I had never experienced such intense desires as I did when I was pregnant.

I remember one evening when I suddenly needed, DO YOU HEAR ME? NEEDED! some chocolate pop and lobster tails. My devoted hubby traversed the countryside and, believe it or not, found me chocolate pop. The lobster tails took an extra day to locate. Then I needed fresh coconuts, which weren't easy to obtain in Michigan during the winter, but Les once again triumphed. My cravings gradually lessened. Actually, I should say they "expanded," because I went from wanting select items to just wanting more of everything, which left me exiting the hospital, after giving birth, the same weight as when I checked in. *Moan.*

When my office manager, Jill, was with child, she sent her bewildered husband, Greg, out at midnight in search of liverwurst and oranges. By the time he found a place open and returned with offerings in hand, her desire for oranges had left as unexpectedly as it had come, while her passion for liverwurst had doubled. Then Jill decided that instead of oranges, she needed orange juice (a drink she had scorned in the past).

During her last pregnancy, my friend Carol went on a Snickers toot. She couldn't seem to get enough chocolate. Trick or treat time was fast approaching, so she stocked up on bags of small candy bars for the neighborhood children. But on Halloween Day, she had to make an emergency run for more candy, because during an intense chocolate frenzy, she had eaten every single piece. Her squishy, brown, chubby fingerprints were all over every empty bag and wrapper.

Wouldn't it be wonderful if we suddenly became deliriously desirous of the Lord? If we developed a ravenous appetite for righteousness? If we craved His ways? If we feasted on His Word? If we thirsted for His will? Then—just think of it—instead of being satiated, we could be satisfied.

"Blessed are the merciful, for they shall receive mercy."

I thought I was a merciful person until I compared my behavior with that of real mercy-givers. Then my mercy paled into niceness. Although appreciated in a cordial way, nice is shallow like a puddle, whereas mercy is deep like a well. Its value cannot be measured in words, for mercy in action is a verb of the richest, highest, and purest kind. Allow me to share with you some "mercy drops" in hopes that some of the mercy might splash over on the rest of us "nice" folks.

When my friend Rose heard of unkind words that had been said against me by a vindictive woman, she wept. Her tears did more for my pain than a thousand condolences could have. Rose extended mercy to me.

My Aunt Pearl, in her late seventies, traveled 600 miles to help our family. She took the all-night shift for weeks, sitting at my mother's bedside in the hospital. Aunt Pearl extended mercy to my mom.

When Carol's son died, her new friend Ruth Manus came to the funeral home and sat quietly for the better part of the day. Her silent vigil was for Carol a strong mercy.

Virginia and Lauren, close friends, gave birth to daughters a short time apart. Lauren became ill, and Virginia became the wet nurse to Lauren's baby. Virginia offered more than her milk to a baby; she extended mercy to a concerned mother.

My friend Lana guided her mother-in-law through the healing of broken relationships before her death to cancer. That was more than being supportive; Lana extended tender mercy.

Don, a friend, was recovering from back surgery and was sitting on the beach, too weak and unsteady to join his friends in the water. One friend noticed Don sitting alone and offered to assist him to the water. Once at the water, the friend held onto Don, steadying him so the waves wouldn't knock him down. Then he helped him back to his towel. This friend extended to Don a hand of mercy.

We lived at a youth camp for several years. One summer, a camper was to receive a three-whack discipline by the camp supervisor for disruptive and disrespectful behavior. But just before the swats were administered, a junior counselor stepped in, took the shaking camper's place, and bore his pain. The young counselor extended to that rebellious boy Christlike mercy.

The "mercy drops" I've listed remind us that mercy goes beyond common courtesy to compassion in action. Mercy extends tender regard to those who are suffering, just as Jesus administered mercy when He freed a frenzied man; wrote a love letter in the sand; spoke to the wanton woman at the well; wept over Jerusalem; consigned His mother's care to John; and then—unselfishly, compassionately, and mercifully—died for us on Calvary's cross.

13

Ampli-
tude

(am´ ple to͞od) n.

Dictionary's definition:
Fullness.

Patsy's definition:
Plenty good.

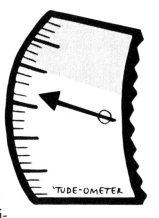

'TUDE-OMETER

Have you ever wished you could be a mouse in the house of someone with a great mind, perhaps Oswald Chambers, Hannah Whitall Smith, or Louisa May Alcott? I actually have had the benefit of traveling and speaking with an exceptional individual, Florence Littauer.

Florence does incredible things with her mind. She uses it, which is what I thought I did with mine until I joined the staff of her Christian Leaders and Speakers Seminars (CLASS), where I served for 10 years. Then I discovered my brain was operating on only one cell . . . sporadically. The rest of my brain cells were evidently out to recess. Florence's cells were not only sitting at their desks paying attention, but they were also prolific.

Florence demonstrated by example the importance of mental agility. She would quiz us, challenge us, and stimulate our interest with visuals, articles, and books. She regaled her staff with her wit and wisdom and had a presence about her that drew the attention and interest of total strangers. She moved through a room with confidence and charisma. Her striking appearance and flamboyant style were only transcended by her wellspring of creativity.

After one particularly exhausting speakers class, we, the staff, stayed on at the hotel for a Christmas party. We all pictured ourselves camping out around the pool and soaking in the Jacuzzi until we shriveled up. Our first morning off we met for breakfast, and then we planned to kick back and relax.

Florence, the Energizer Bunny, had other ideas. She handed out job descriptions to each of us for the party that evening. Job descriptions? We had just planned to show up and eat. Instead, however, she sent us off to the mall with partners to collect all the items necessary for our part in the Christmas celebration.

Francine Jackson and I were assigned to give out awards to each staff person. "Awards? For what?" we asked Florence. She smiled and, with a twinkle in her eye, said, "That's up to the two of you." Puzzled and frazzled, we grumbled our way over to the mall.

At first, Francine and I were like two walking blanks. But when we started to move out of our tired 'tude and into our assignment, our creativity began to flow. With the ideas came something else unexpected—energy and excitement. We laughed at our award choices and giggled over how we would present them. Soon we were buzzing around the stores, having a grand time. Once we completed our scavenger hunt, we had just enough time to hurry back to our room, wrap the awards, and dress for dinner.

When we entered our private dining quarters for the evening, our mouths fell open at the splendor of the room. The candles on the tables illuminated the golden apple sitting on each plate; wrapped gifts glittered; and we had our very own chef. It was obvious Florence had put a great deal of thought into this event.

After a fabulous, flaming meal, the program began. We laughed until we cried at the poems, titles, awards, and especially the music. Lana Bateman and Barbara Bueler, two classmates, selected old songs to portray personality temperaments and then acted them out. They were hilarious, and we saw a side of Lana and Barbara we had never seen before. I think they surprised even themselves.

By the time the evening was over, I was so relaxed and renewed that I was sorry to see it end. It was truly one of the most delightful parties I had ever attended, and all because Florence had challenged us to think and act creatively. She put stretch marks on our brains and left imprints on our hearts. I learned that the more effort I'm willing to invest, the greater the result and the sweeter the memory.

During the years I was involved in CLASS, each seminar day we would break into small groups. As a group leader, I had the joy of watching men and women develop their communication skills. One way we mentally stretched the groups was to give each participant an ad from a magazine and to challenge the student to develop a speech around the ad, including an example from his or her life. Often the class would look at us wide-eyed, certain they couldn't do this. We only gave them five minutes to prepare, and they had to speak for three minutes.

Again and again, however, as the group participants risked thinking in ways they hadn't experienced before, they were thrilled with the results. Many times they would ask to keep their ads to show others and as a reminder for themselves that they were capable of spontaneous mental creativity and clarity, if not downright brilliance.

Our brains can think more, retain more, and process more than we realize. But just as our bodies get flimsy without exercise, so do our minds. Let's try some mental gymnastics to see if we can't firm up and use the ol' cranial for something other than a hat rack (as my dad would say).

How long has it been since you've read a classic? What about taking a course at your local night school? Have you added any new words to your vocabulary lately? (*Samovar* is my newest.) Try some difficult crossword puzzles. Do a study on the life of the apostle Paul. (Did you know Paul was stout, bald, and bowlegged?) Memorize Psalm 100, the Ten Commandments, and the Sermon on the Mount. Teach a Sunday school class. Learn the basics of a new language. Read a book a month for six months. Then write reviews of them and pass on the positive reviews to encourage others to read. (Keep a copy of your reviews. A good book, like a good friend, is worth remembering.)

Visit a museum or an art gallery. Attend a ballet, an opera, or a play, and don't forget to take in a symphony. (A symphony is a bubble bath for the brain.) Have a brainstorming session with someone you respect about a stuck place in your life or a new endeavor. Write a poem, a song, your will, a book (everyone has at least one book in him or her—just ask Florence). Plan a trip on paper, and then take it. Talk to an elderly person; visit with a child; hold an infant. Then write down what you learned from the experience. Invest what you know in an eager recipient. Let someone younger teach you something. Write a children's story, and then find a child to read it to. Allow him or her to critique it.

There really is no end to amplitude opportunities. In fact, why don't you make your own list and act on it? Perhaps one day someone will want to be a mouse in your house!

14

Certi-*tude*

(sur´ té tōōd) n.

Dictionary's definition:
Complete assurance.

Patsy's definition:
"I told you so."

Have you ever been certain about something or someone, only to be surprised later by a change of heart, a turn of events, or a new revelation? As a young girl, I believed birds stayed dry in the rain by standing in between the drops. My daddy told me

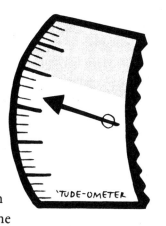

'TUDE-OMETER

that. He also said I could catch a bird if I put salt on its tail. It didn't take long, about one box of Morton's, before I realized my dad was spoofing me. It has taken me much longer to sort out other misconceptions.

My husband and his siblings grew up in a poor and difficult environment. Their childhood lifestyle was very different from the ease of mine. Often I sat spellbound as I listened to them describe their family adventures. One time, Les mentioned that they were so poor (How poor were they?) that their dad rubbed bacon grease on their faces before they left for school so people would think they had eaten breakfast. Just call me gullible, but I believed it for years.

I believed getting married would end all my problems. A week after the wedding, fact turned into fallacy when I realized Les expected me to cook. Then I was sure children were the solution for marital bliss and personal harmony. Six weeks of our baby's colic cured that certainty. I knew owning a car would bring us a sense of well-being. Two weeks later, our new-used car blew an engine, and I blew a gasket. Certainty was fast becoming uncertain.

I know I'm not the only one who has felt this way. Ask little Anne Wallis. She went to her first day of kindergarten certain of what to expect. Things went her way until the end of the day. Then her teacher announced it was time to pick up all the toys. A frown fell over Anne's face as she headed for the teacher. "Miss Ruth," Anne said with her southern drawl and an air of five-year-old authority, "I'm Anne Wallis, and I don't do pick-up."

Well, Miss Ruth and little Miss Anne Wallis had a heart-to-heart discussion regarding Anne's 'tude, wherein she was assured by her teacher that her kindergarten future *would* include "pick-up."

I'm on Anne's side. In fact, there are a lot of "up" phrases that feel down: pick up, give up, time's up, get up, throw up, grow up, and shut up. Yet I can say with certainty I've done them all. (Well, I'm still working on one of them. Okay, maybe two.) Anyway, just about the time we think we're certain about "things," somebody changes the script.

My niece Susan assisted with a singing group at her church. Called the Music Sprouts, the singers were three- and four-year-olds. The song they learned was "Praise Ye the Lord." Gratefully, it was a song of few words and constant repetition, making it easier for everyone to memorize. After practice one evening, Susan heard a little sprout practicing her lines as she left the church. In her clearest voice she sang, "Crazy the Lord, hallelujah! Crazy the Lord, hallelujah!"

Sometimes when I'm not certain what the Lord is doing, I sing that same song. The Lord is unpredictable; you can almost predict it. I remember the time I developed a mysterious cough. I sounded like a wounded seal in labor with triplets. My cough registered a

7.2 on the Richter scale. It became so debilitating that I couldn't even lie down to sleep but had to be propped up with pillows. All night, as I tried to snooze in an upright position, my head bobbed around as if I were dunking for apples.

This bobbing and barking had been going on for about three months (Les was ready to mount me on his dashboard) when a lady in a restaurant heard my cough, came up, and told me she was certain she could help me. She then insisted I come by her place and try a natural remedy she had.

I nodded my head in consent on the outside, but I shook my head "no" on the inside. I had already tried more weird concoctions than I had previously known existed. Besides, she wasn't a believer, so how could she help me? I was certain that if the Lord wanted to help me, He would use one of His own—thank you.

But somehow we ended up at her doorstep. She handed me a bottle of teensy Ping-Pong-ball pills to be held under my tongue. I envisioned slam-dunking them into the garbage when I got home. Then, as if she had read my mind, she opened the bottle and spilled several into my hand to take in front of her. I hadn't counted on that. I reluctantly ingested them, took the bottle, and left murmuring.

I was certain iridescent flowers would sprout from my ears in reaction to the strange medication. Instead, however, within a few hours, Les noticed I wasn't coughing as much and suggested I take more of the pills. I did.

In two days, I was well. I was breathing normally, sleeping horizontally, and finally free of my hacking cough. Who would have thunk it: a nonbeliever used by the Lord for one of His own. "Crazy the Lord, hallelujah!"

Come to think of it, wasn't that the theme song of the Israelites, the Pharisees, and some others who couldn't figure out what unpredictable

God was up to? Why, take a look at poor, baffled Gideon. He was a young man who learned he was God's choice to lead his people into battle. Shaken at having been selected for this post, Gideon whipped out a current résumé to prove how unqualified he was.

The angel, undaunted, commanded Gideon to stand tall in his own strength.

Gideon then asked the angel for *his* résumé. Gideon was certain one of them was crazy. After all, he knew for certain that he had been sneaking around to hide from the enemy, so why had the angel of the Lord referred to him as a valiant soldier? (I think the confusion here was that Gideon looked back on what *was*, while the angel looked forward to what *would be*.)

The angel of God responded to Gideon's need for proof by creating a consuming fire on a rock. Then he disappeared and spoke without a human form to Gideon.

Now, I don't know about you, but that would have been enough proof for me. In fact, forget the fire. One flick of that angel's Bic and I would have signed on the dotted line. Actually Gideon did, for a while. But then he lapsed into uncertainty—I think he wanted to be sure no one was pulling the fleece over his eyes—and made extreme requests of the Lord. (Check out Gideon's wet-wool/dry-wool tangent in Judges 6:36-40.)

The Lord not only answered Gideon's requests, but He also responded with a few unusual requests of His own. You might say the angel asked Gideon to take potshots at the enemy, for his soldiers were armed not with Uzis but with trumpets, empty pots, and torches to place inside the pots (pitchers). If ever there was a time to sing "Crazy the Lord," that would seem to have been it. (I know I'd have been humming a few bars.)

But surprisingly, once Gideon took his place as leader, the men followed him into battle. They honked their horns, flashed their lights, and sang, "For the Lord and Gideon." They caused such a ruckus that the enemy created its own deadly traffic jam.

My, my, the Lord certainly has His ways. And I've noticed they certainly don't seem to be our ways. I guess it's not so important for us to be certain of what or how the Lord will perform His will, but just to be certain He will.

I do understand Gideon's reluctance to believe the best when he felt he was the worst. In my twenties, I was not only an agoraphobic, but I was also addicted to tranquilizers, caffeine, and nicotine. I smoked two packs of cigarettes a day for years. After becoming a believer, I wanted to quit, but my addiction was strong, and I was weak. I repeatedly asked the Lord to deliver me, but it wasn't happening.

Then there came a voice from heaven. No, it wasn't the angel of the Lord, but it was nonetheless an angel (unaware). My Jewish friend Louie said to me, "You're using all your strength to give up smoking. Don't worry about the cigarettes. Instead, take that strength and use it to fall more deeply in love with Jesus, and one day the cigarettes will give *you* up."

Following my talk with Louie, I attended Bible studies, church, and women's retreats, nurturing my love for Jesus. Then it happened . . . I was certain it was time.

I was at a friend's house, and I told Rose the cigarettes were ready to give me up. She called to Daryl, another friend, to join us in the kitchen. Rose then announced that we would pray, but first we would anoint me with oil. She checked her cupboard and found she was out of oil. "Not to worry," Rose said, because she had a can of Crisco. She scooped out a dollop on her finger and splatted it onto my forehead. (Do you know what happens when Crisco meets body heat?) I felt like a french fry. Rose then offered to lead the prayer. My thought was, *Good. While she prays, I'll dab the*

Crisco from my drippy eyebrows. Then she and Daryl placed their hands on my shoulders and prayed. And I never smoked again.

What a strange service! But I guess that if the Lord could use pots and trumpets for Gideon's victory, He could certainly use a kitchen and Crisco for giddy me. Praise ye the Lord!

The next time you discover certitude has turned into uncertainty, you might try humming a few bars of "Crazy the Lord." It will remind you that what at first crazes us can turn into praises to Him. Of that you can be certain.

Longi-*tude*

(län´ je to͞od) n.

Dictionary's definition:
Measurable distance.

Patsy's definition:
The long and lonely distance
between two hearts.

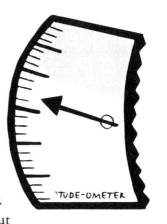

'TUDE-OMETER

I live in a small but fast-growing community. Our house is close to downtown on a lovely, tree-lined street. Our modest home sits nestled among similar houses. My immediate neighbors are warm and friendly. We often chat over our fences about the weather, our flowers, and our families. My loving husband is usually at my side, and our grown sons are, gratefully, a constant part of our lives. My phone rings endlessly, and I've been blessed with many friends. My mailbox is often plump with thoughtful cards and notes. So how, with wonderful people surrounding me, could I ever feel a long, lonely distance between myself and others? Yet at times I do.

Loneliness for me is like a dull ache, a sadness, a feeling of being forgotten. It feels as if I'm calling for help down a long, empty hall. When I'm lonely, I feel misunderstood, neglected, and separate. I'm then a prime candidate for self-pity to come visiting. Actually, it's more than a visit, for self-pity brings her endless supply of tissues and becomes a sniveling houseguest, uninvited yet indulged.

How is it that so many people (6 billion) live on earth, and yet longitudes are one of our greatest emotional and relational battles?

It's certainly not a new battle, but it seems that as time goes by and our population enlarges, the distance between us only increases. You would think that the more people who inhabit the world, the less loneliness there would be. *Unless loneliness isn't caused or resolved by people.* Hmm.

Could it be that loneliness began when Adam and Eve opted to go their own way? I wonder if the ache within could be a call to our hearts to turn toward Home? Perhaps loneliness is a scary siren to remind us that people are unable, try as they might, to move close enough to ease our deep discomfort and disconnection. If that's so, is it possible that loneliness is actually an evangelist, a teacher, even a friend?

The evangelistic side of loneliness reminds us that only One hears our unspoken words, and that our unformed thoughts are in His conscious awareness. The teacher part of loneliness points out our inability to draw sufficient comfort from others or ourselves in these forlorn moments. The friend in loneliness might try to convince us that in and of ourselves we're insufficient, but our sufficiency is in Christ.

Loneliness has the potential to guide us to the friend who is able to stick closer than a brother. But potential can turn to poison when, instead of responding to truth, we indulge our loneliness until it becomes a melancholy mind-set, a distorted way of thinking, seeing, and feeling. At times we entertain our sadness and become dependent on our despondency to extend to us a sick sort of comfort.

I took a spontaneous poll at our local eatery, Lynn's Cafe, this afternoon. I asked the owner and her family, workers, and patrons when they were most aware of being lonely. They all agreed the pangs were greatest when they were with others rather than when they were by themselves.

One of the customers said, "There's no type of loneliness more painful than when you're married and feel alone while in the presence of your mate."

To that one gal replied, "I was talking with a single friend, and she was saying she felt lonely. I told her that when you're alone you expect at times to feel that way. But when you're married, you anticipate your mate will fill that empty place. When he can't or won't, it's more devastating than being by yourself."

What I heard them say is that a deafening distance can exist between two people even in the same house, the same room, the same bed. Also, people are limited, by desire and design, in what they can do to relieve each other's inner emptiness.

I wonder if that's how David felt (empty) when he had been deserted by friends turned foe. David cried out to the Lord, "Turn to me" (Ps. 25:16). It sounds as if David felt not only a long distance away from God, but also that God had turned His attention elsewhere and was unaware of David's dilemma. David continued, "For I am lonely and afflicted." I guess we all feel abandoned when we're under attack, especially when we're persecuted unfairly.

Paul knew about persecution and loneliness from both sides of the fence. For he (Saul) not only persecuted others for their faith, but he (Paul—new name) also suffered at the hands of others for his faith. Perhaps it was in lonely moments that he wrote, "For our citizenship is in heaven, from which also we eagerly wait for a Savior, the Lord Jesus Christ" (Phil. 3:20), and "We . . . prefer rather to be absent from the body and to be at home with the Lord" (2 Cor. 5:8).

At some point in his dramatic life, Paul realized we weren't going to be at home totally (even with ourselves) until we stepped on heaven's shore. Then the disturbing distance between us and others would disappear. Any disconnected feeling between us and the Lord would be over, and our inner and outer struggles with loneliness would be eternally resolved.

Until then, we need to keep on keeping on. It's not easy to carry on when you're feeling alone, which is why it's important to expect to feel separation at times (from God, others, and ourselves) as part of our fallen condition. That way, the long-distance times can't sneak up on us and leave us distraught, but we can lean into our loneliness and learn.

Jesus promised never to leave us, and He is a promise keeper. Our times of loneliness don't testify to His absence in our lives, but rather the loneliness allows us to feel our human dilemma (of limitations) from which only He can rescue us. The Lord didn't say He would shelter us from the full range of human emotions, from joy to devastation and from sweet fellowship to acute loneliness. Our emotions don't alter God's constancy in our lives. Instead, negative emotions often prompt us to search out the positive principles of His unfailing presence.

One of the tender artistic portrayals of Christ as shepherd that stands out in my mind is entitled "Lost Lamb." The artist shows Christ as He leans over the side of a cliff and extends His shepherd's crook around a bewildered lamb on a ledge. You know He will then draw the lonely creature into the safety of His arms.

The next time you feel lost and lonely, remember there is One who longs for you to know you're not alone. The good Shepherd knows you by name, and He will travel the long distance on your behalf. He will search the widest pasture, the steepest highlands, the deepest valley, and even the most desolate desert to help you find your way, so intense is His love for you.

Inepti-*tude*

(in ept´ e tōōd) n.

Dictionary's definition:
Unsuitable.

Patsy's definition:
Oops!

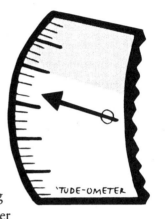

'TUDE-OMETER

After repeated episodes of Marvin's garbage being ripped apart by some varmint, Marvin just wanted the vandalism to stop. Then one evening, he took the garbage out, and—aha—a raccoon was hot-footing it for the big maple out front. Marv, being a hunter from way back, instinctively grabbed his bow and arrows with the thought of ending the mania of this midnight marauder.

Marv took aim, and the arrow took flight. It hit the masked scavenger but didn't finish him off. Marv, who was usually an accurate marksman, was concerned because he didn't want the scamp to suffer needlessly. He shot a couple more times, but now his target darted higher into the tree, and Marv had trouble seeing through the leaves. The neighbors weren't having any trouble seeing, however, and what they saw they didn't like. Evidently they thought Marv was the Big Bad Wolf and the raccoon was Little Red Riding Hood. The neighbors called in reinforcements.

When the police arrived, no one was more surprised than Marv, who thought he was ridding the neighborhood of a rascal. Well, the policeman must have had a soft spot for raccoons, because he thought Marv was the rascal. Within a short time, the animal protection people were on the scene, as well as the fire department, which had arrived with a ladder rig to assist in the rescue of Little Red Riding Hood. A crowd from the surrounding homes formed. People took turns pointing at the Big Bad Wolf, who was now seated in the back of the patrol car.

After repeated attempts to rescue the raccoon failed (the coon had climbed beyond the reach of the ladder), a cherry picker from the city was called in. And the woman from the animal protection group set up a tent under the tree to spend the night in case they couldn't reach the raccoon before morning.

Marv felt stuck in a bad dream. But he woke up when the police slapped him with a ticket. It was now midnight, and a police car, a fire truck, an animal rights vehicle, a cherry picker, and a disgruntled crowd stood in front of his home. Finally, the coon was caught and Marv was released.

But Marv's story didn't end there. No, he still had to go to court and pay fines and the city's cost in sending out vehicles. Then there was the newspaper article informing the community of his misdeed.

Oh, by the way, the Big Bad Wolf turned out to be a sheep in wolf's clothing. Marv was the pastor of the church I attend. You can only imagine what kind of complications this brought him ("a man of the cloth caught cooning"). Marvin contritely went before the church and apologized for any embarrassment he had brought on the congregation. He said that in retrospect, he realized he hadn't thought through his action and hadn't imagined the uproar it would cause. His choice to pursue the raccoon, he confessed, was inept.

Marvin is one of the dearest, sincerest, and funniest men you would ever want to meet. He handled his humiliation with appropriate regret and then took a tremendous amount of ribbing from the congregation. In time, the scandal settled down (yes, we live in a small town). But have you ever noticed that the thing you wish people would forget is what seems to linger in their minds?

Some months later, it was Marv's fiftieth birthday, and the church put on a surprise shindig for him. At one point during the hoopla, we blindfolded Marv, and my husband, Les, came out in a raccoon suit carrying a bow and arrow. The group guffawed, stomped the floor, and beat on the tables until everyone was almost sick. Marv was still blindfolded and chuckling as he tried to imagine what riotous thing was occurring.

Finally, we uncovered his eyes just as Super Coon drew back his bow and pointed it in Marv's direction. Good-natured Marv spotted the 200-pound raccoon and bent over to give the raccoon an ample target. What fun we had that night as we let our pastor know he was loved and that we realized we're all inept at times!

Marv wore his mistake well. He wasn't defensive, he didn't deny his actions, and he took responsibility in court and in church. After years of chiding, he has kept up his chin but not his back.

My back was up so high recently that I was five inches taller than usual. Les and I had just parked our car in a mall parking area. Because of my husband's severe health issues, we have a handicap permit, but Les doesn't *look* handicapped. As we stepped out of our car, a woman walking toward the store suddenly turned around and said, "Did you know that's a handicap spot?"

Immediately my hackles went up, and I responded, "We certainly do."

"Well, I don't see your permit," she said accusingly.

"Well, it's there," I snapped, and then added, "and we've had it for years."

The woman took a couple of steps toward the door and then turned back and said, "You know, you really shouldn't get angry. You should be grateful I'm checking."

"I do understand your concern," I replied, "but I felt your tone was accusatory."

She and I continued to walk toward the store, and then she turned and said, "If you'd hang your handicap tag from your mirror instead of laying it on your dash, people wouldn't have to challenge you."

Certain I should have the last word, I shot back, "I think it's up to my husband where he places his tag." With that I marched away, and she headed in a huff in another direction.

I hadn't taken five steps when I stopped, realizing I had just experienced a major ineptitude episode, and I needed to do something pronto. I knew if I waited even a few minutes, I would lose that woman and possibly never have the chance to take responsibility for my behavior. I spotted her and started down an aisle in her direction. She saw me coming and seemed to grow taller in preparation. When I reached her I said, "You were right, and I shouldn't have been so defensive. There was no reason for that. And we'll take your suggestion under consideration."

As I started to walk away, I heard her say quietly, "Thank you."

What a brouhaha I had created! All I needed to say when she asked if we had a permit was "Yes, we do." Then I could have reminded Les to hang up his permit. "A soft answer turneth away wrath, but grievous words stir up anger" (Prov. 15:1, KJV).

I doubt that woman has had half as much trouble forgiving me as I've had forgiving myself. I'm 50, not 15. I know better than to behave so ineptly.

Perhaps my trigger personality is why I've always had compassion for the disciple Peter. I feel as if I've walked in his hyper-sandals. Talk about inept! Peter couldn't take two steps without tripping over his tongue. His words and actions often slipped out past his better judgment. He either said too much or not enough. Or worse yet, in a fit of fury, he would rearrange people's anatomies, like the time he lopped off the Roman soldier's ear.

I'm reminded of Alexander Pope's description, "a brain of feathers and a heart of lead." Gratefully, Peter had a lot of heart—no lead there. I'd like to think I have a big heart, too. But about the other, well, I guess if the feathers fit, we have to wear them—at least until we purpose to think before we speak and act. That's not to say that even thinking will always keep us from being, looking, or sounding inept. Sometimes our information is just plain faulty.

Greta Propps waited eagerly for the principal to call her name for her junior high school diploma and outstanding student award. This was an exciting moment as she looked forward to entering high school. The long line in front of her at the commencement services slowly diminished until finally, it was her moment to rise and shine. The principal cleared his throat and succinctly announced her name into the microphone: "Gurta Poops." Well, the audience loved it. The principal was stymied by the crowd's response. And "Gurta" almost lived up to her name. But the principal had read correctly. Somebody, ineptly, had typed Greta's name wrong not only on the list of graduating students, but also on her trophy. Imagine displaying that *faux pas* for future generations.

Making an honest mistake with a name is one thing, but trying to make a raccoon into a pincushion (like Marv), a stranger into an enemy (like Patsy), or a guard into a hearing aid candidate (like Peter) are more deliberate and blatant forms of ineptitude. It becomes harder for others to forgive our foolishness and extremely difficult for us to forgive ourselves.

I love the picture of Jesus when He looked back at Peter after he had betrayed Him. I believe it was not a look of condemnation but one of deep compassion. Peter left the Lord's gaze devastated by his own ineptitude. After the resurrection, however, Jesus sent back a special message to Peter so that he might be assured of his place in the Savior's heart.

I'm grateful Peter wasn't perfect, because I identify with his flighty, forceful personality. Peter is like a message of hope from the Savior for all of us who experience ineptitude. We are loved, `tudes and all.

Simili-*tude*

(sim´ e le tōōd) n.

Dictionary's definition:
Resemblance.

Patsy's definition:
Mirror, mirror on the wall.

My friend Carol and I have similar interests. We're both antique buffs (not to mention we're both antiques), and we enjoy our collections of teapots and cookbooks, our artistic endeavors, entertaining children, and eating Finnish pastries. But if you were to compare our physical similarities, there aren't any. Carol is a skyscraper, and I'm a scanty shanty. Carol has enormous eyes; they're about the size of coconut pies. My eyes are slim slits similar to those of a cat-napping Siamese. Carol has an elongated, casual stride. I take short, snappy steps. We also are dissimilar in our personalities. Carol is reticent. I'm loquacious. Carol looks for others to take the lead. I could have been a dictator. So even though we share a similitude in some areas, we're very different.

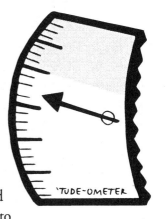

'TUDE-OMETER

My son Jason and I look like tic and tac. My son Marty and my husband, Les, look like bric and brac. Jason and I are fair-skinned, blue-eyed blonds. Marty and Les are darker-skinned, with brown hair and brown-and-hazel eyes. In our family pictures, we look like two sets of bookends.

When Jason was in high school, I went with him to attend a program for parents. I was concerned it would embarrass him if I walked at his side, so I offered to trail in after him. He said, "It won't matter, Mom; one look at you and everyone will know we belong together anyway." It was true; we're that similar.

But a closer examination would tell you how opposite we are. Jason has a hammock mind (slow and easy), whereas I'm more of a blender brain (lots of thoughts spinning around, all mixed together). Jason avoids conflict, and I'm challenged by it. He's naturally cautious, while I'm given to spontaneity. His favorite word is *chill*. Mine is *thrill*. We're similar; yet we're different.

I like being my own unique person, although I long to be similar and to connect with others. It's often a relief when someone else admits to a fault that I have but haven't admitted (like overdosing on Godiva chocolates). It sounds as if misery loves company, but it's more, because relating, even in a fault, gives a sense of belonging and normality. Yet as much as we need to identify closely with others, we fight to maintain our distinctiveness. Aren't we a peculiar lot?

When Carol and I were growing up, we would often wear matching outfits, except we would buy them in different colors. (There's that struggle again; we want to be like others . . . sorta.) One summer, we both bought beach hats, and even though we couldn't stand for the other to have a hat unless we did, too, we couldn't bring ourselves to buy identical hats. Carol's looked like a spaceship, while mine looked like the landing pad. Similar, yet, well, you know . . . different.

My friend Ann tells of being at the mall with her husband, Paul. It was crowded, and they were moving through the crowds, window-gazing as they walked. Ann glanced into a store and then turned back and took Paul's hand. As she did, she looked up at Paul, only to find she was holding the hand of a stranger! Shocked and embarrassed, she tossed the startled man's hand as if it were a hot coal and turned to find Paul casually strolling behind her.

Hands can look so similar.

My mom, Rebecca, had three sisters, Elvira, Hazel, and Pearl. Not surprisingly, because they were sisters, their hands looked alike, with plump fingers. They were hands that knew work, hard work as well as healing work. Those eight hands touched many lives—not only their families', but also friends', neighbors', co-workers', and patients'. Each was her own dynamic person, but they all connected with others at an important level, the level of human need. Those sisters shared a similitude by the way they extended their hands to help those less fortunate.

At a weekend retreat I attended in the South, I was aware of a small cluster of women as they entered. Three of the gals were similar in appearance. They interacted freely and extended themselves warmly to others. But the fourth woman in the group didn't resemble the others and stood off to the side, uninvolved.

The oldest woman was a hands-on gal, a real hugger. She enthusiastically worked her way around the room, hugging everyone as she went. She seemed to sincerely care for others, and I looked forward to meeting her. Sure enough, when I did, I received a hug, too. It was one of those big-momma hugs, the kind that says you're loved and prayed for, the kind that makes you want to behave.

I found out later that the two similar young women were her daughters. The hesitant gal was her daughter-in-law. The energetic mom continued through the retreat to reach out compassionately to those around her, as did her delightful daughters. The daughter-in-law stayed physically near to her family while maintaining an emotional distance from everyone.

After my closing session, the mother came to me in tears. She said that as she had stood up to leave the retreat, she had turned to retrieve her sweater off the back of her chair and had noticed her daughter-in-law seated behind her, crying. "Now," she said to me, "you may not think that's a big deal, but this girl has been in our family for eight years, and we've never seen her shed a tear. When she married my son, I was excited, because she was an orphan and I was a mother with more love than I knew what to do with. I was certain the Lord had brought us together so that I might give her the mother's love she had never known. But she wasn't interested in my affection or my willingness to nurture her. Year after year I've reached out to her, and she has resisted all my attempts.

"When I saw her crying today, I found myself risking another rejection as I moved toward her to comfort her. I was certain that once again she would push me away. But instead, as I encircled her with my arms, she fell into them and sobbed. I held her and rocked her. When her sobbing eased into teardrops, she looked up at me and said, 'Oh, Momma, I love you.'"

What a sweet time of rejoicing we had as we celebrated this loving breakthrough! Their differences had separated them, love connected them, and for the first time, the mother-in-law and daughter-in-law became family emotionally.

Since that day, I have often thought of the tenaciousness of that little mother-in-law who didn't give up on her daughter-in-law but hung in for the long haul. No one would have blamed her if she had thrown up her hands in frustration after eight years of rejection and walked away from the relationship. But instead, she waited out her daughter-in-law, then extended her hands, not to push away her daughter-in-law, but to draw her in, close to that big mother's heart. The wall of differences was broken down by the power of love.

It was interesting to me that, as the mother and daughter-in-love walked away, they now looked so, so . . . similar. Somehow the new beginning in their relationship had brought about a transformation even in their appearances.

When my son Jason was seven, I noticed one day that he was studying me closely. "Mom," he said, "do you know who I think of when I look at you?"

Amused and interested, I asked, "No, who?"

"Me," he quickly responded.

Wouldn't it be glorious if one day our heavenly Father told us we had become so conformed, so similar to His Son that when He looked at us, He was reminded of Himself?

18

Vicissi-*tude*

(vi sis′ e to͞od) n.

Dictionary's definition:
Change.

Patsy's definition:
Discombobulate.

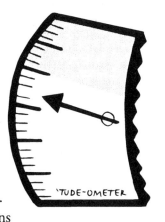

'TUDE-OMETER

Change jobs, change tires, change diapers, change doctors, change directions, change addresses, change underwear, change hair color—change, change, change. The world is in flux—just ask my dog, Pumpkin. Pumpkin is in menopause, which means exactly that, men-oh-*pause*. She's very touchy. Just ask my nephew Nicholas. He made the mistake of kissing her when she wasn't in the mood. Warning! Warning! Do not, I repeat, *do not* do that to a woman in flux. Nicholas now wears a small memento of that occasion on his cheek, and it's not lipstick.

I know Pumpkin is in her change, because she has little growling spells even when no one is near her. She also insists on going outside far more frequently than before. Once on the lawn, she can't seem to remember why she's out there. The other day, she turned around in circles 22 times before she found an acceptable blade of grass to receive her offering—definitely a sign of menopausal indecision. Also, hair is sprouting out of her ears, the skin on her tummy has funny things growing on it, her coat has thinned, her skin has thickened, she has gained weight, and she's always tired. Yep, as I said, this dog's going through her change.

I wonder why change always seems to come with a price tag. I know I find it costly when I change locations as frequently as I do. I often fly back and forth across the country changing time zones, weather conditions, water supplies, and types of food. These variations keep my body and mind topsy-turvy, not to mention my stomach.

One day last spring, I rose early to take a flight to Dallas. I was feeling strange. By the time I left for the airport, Les and I were both aware I had the flu. We grabbed a Hefty bag for any emergency that might arise on the drive. We arrived at Detroit Metro, and halfway through the airport, everyone around me became aware I was not well. We were all grateful I had come equipped for an emergency.

I should have gone home and straight to bed, but for some reason I can't explain, I thought if I could just get to my destination, I'd be fine. I didn't want to change my plans if I could help it. Les reluctantly watched me stagger onto the plane as I embraced a new Hefty.

Ten minutes into the flight, I realized it would be in everyone's best interest if I took up residence in the rest room. Which I did. Knowing I couldn't stay indefinitely, however, after a lengthy visit, I stepped out and found myself face to face with a flight attendant. She took one look at me and insisted I take her jump seat next to the bathroom. Which I did. (Maybe she was hoping I'd jump.)

Now, either flyers were distributed on the plane telling of the sickee aboard, or my pasty-white skin fringed in vivid green was the giveaway. Whatever the reason, every passenger who wanted to use the rest room would look at me for consent before entering. I would lower my eyelids once for yes or knock them back three aisles (as I bolted for the cubicle) for no.

At one point, a male attendant knelt next to me and told me he had talked with my son before the flight had left Detroit. I muttered,

"How nice, but that was my husband." Then the attendant looked kind of green. I was so ill I didn't even mind his flub . . . although I did breathe on him before disembarking.

By the time I arrived at the hotel, I had one goal—go to bed and never get up. I was too sick to speak that night or the next morning. I could have helped my situation if I had just stayed home. Then I at least could have taken care of myself and not risked spreading my affliction. But the last-minute change would have inconvenienced many people, and I didn't want to pay the price of disappointing anyone. So instead I showed up looking and feeling as if I had the bubonic plague and ultimately disappointed people anyway.

Change is difficult, whether it's changing locations or changing our minds.

We've often heard it said, "These are changing times." Actually, times have always been changing. Times are different for my adult children than they were for me, just as my times were different from my mom's, whose were different from her mom's.

My Mamaw (grandmother), Thanie Elizabeth Griffin McEuen, walked on this earth's turf for more than 97 years. She was born in the horse-and-buggy days and lived to see men on the moon. Even though her world saw radical changes, Thanie still found personal change difficult.

I remember family members had to do a heap of talkin' to get Mamaw to give up her icebox and buy a refrigerator. Those newfangled things didn't seem that necessary to her. And that was her approach toward most new things that would alter what she was used to. I never did succeed in getting her to wear a pair of slacks. Her spindly little legs were always freezing, and I thought slacks would warm her right up. But she had never worn a pair in her life and didn't plan to start at this late date, "thank ye kindly."

Thanie stuck to her ways a bit too emphatically one time when she was going to stay at my parents' home for an extended visit. She came out of her house carrying her chamber jar. My mom is hospitable, but not that hospitable. Mamaw and my dad had quite a debate over that piece of porcelain before he finally convinced her we had a sufficient water closet to meet her needs.

I guess vicissitude can be scary, because change does have an uncertain (I don't know what's going to happen) element to it. Our younger son, Jason, was married last September to a beautiful young woman named Danya. We were excited and happy for the newlyweds, but in the back of my mind, I knew I would be faced for the first time in 30 years with an empty nest. No doubt about it, an empty nest is different—not bad, but different. I confess, though, that I did have a couple of misty moments as the long-term reality settled in.

My friend Nancy was a big promoter of the notion that when a young person graduates from high school, you should present him or her with a sack lunch and a road map. She had been telling me for years: When kids are old enough, let them experience life. Nudge (or shove) them out of the nest, and let them fly.

Then it came time for her only son, Matt, to graduate from high school, and he chose to attend a college in the East. Nancy was delighted. The change didn't bother her in the least . . . until she was walking through the grocery store a couple of days after he had left and she spotted his favorite cereal. Then she lost it.

Nancy's husband, David, came home from work that day and found Nancy slumped over her son's bed, weeping. The change in change caught her off guard.

Nancy and I have since giggled about how easy it is to theorize, but theory is a long emotional distance from reality. And the reality is, change often comes with a painful transitional period.

Dorcas was trying to help her 11-year-old son, Jacob, transition from childish actions to responsible behavior. He was a delightful boy, but Dorcas was having trouble getting him to turn off the light in his room before leaving for school. In her attempts to convince him to change, she tried a number of creative tactics, but repeatedly when she passed his room, he would be gone, and the light would be on.

One day, she had had it. Dorcas let Jacob know he would suffer some nasty consequences if his light wasn't turned off before he left that day. Satisfied she had made her point, she busied herself until she heard him leave. Once he was out the door, she made a beeline upstairs to see if he had finally responded to her demands. To her relief and amazement, the light was off. And then she began to giggle. Jacob had turned out his *overhead* light, but he had left on his closet light, the hall light, the night light, and the bathroom light. Dorcas said, "Jacob obeyed the letter of the law while totally destroying the spirit."

I've been there, Jacob. I, too, have done what I felt forced to do, but not in the most honorable way. I've apologized in a snarling fashion because I felt I had to and not because I wanted to take responsibility. I've done a good deed because it was expected rather than from a caring heart. I've acted sweet while sportin' an acidic 'tude. More times than I'd like to believe, I've done the right thing in the wrong way.

That brings us to the most important change of all—the change of the human heart.

We can change a number of things in this life, but many we can't. Our heart is a can't. Try as we might to be good and do right, we fall miserably short of wholeness or holiness without Jesus. The wonderful news is He will not only change our hearts at our invitation, but He will also help us through unavoidable changes. He will assist us with the cost of change, the uncertainty of change, and the adjustments necessary during change, whether that be the ticking of our biological clocks, unexpected health issues, or feeling the pangs of watching our last little chicks sprout wings and fly. That's good news for a change, don't you think?

19

Loony **'Tudes**

(lōō′ nē tōōds) n.

Dictionary's definition:
Strange and unusual.

Patsy's definition:
My kooky comrades.

I'm convinced that the Lord, who created us in His own image, laughs. And I'm certain He meant for us to laugh until we cry as an emotional safety valve. He knew life would pile up inside us, and a sense of humor would help us to shovel our way out of

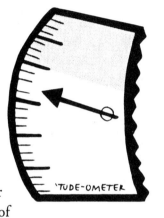

our serious circumstances. At times, laughter must be as sweet an offering to Him as tears and even prayers.

My mom and her sisters didn't believe in foolishness, but they sure believed in a good time. They worked hard and laughed hard. I always looked forward to being with them, even as a child. The smell of down-home cooking and the sound of good-hearted laughter were an unforgettable combination.

I have been blessed to have not only a heritage and a husband of humor, but also a passel of loony 'tude friends. They've helped me survive when life knocked the humor out of me or when I took myself too seriously. Laughter puts life back in its temporal position, lest we think our earthly stint is all there is to this journey. Also, shared laughter leads to an emotional connection with others.

I remember attending a large conference where I noticed a couple of my long-lost friends seated in a row near the front. I decided to join them, which meant I would have to climb over several of them to reach the empty seat. That didn't seem to be a problem—and probably wouldn't have been had I not gained weight.

Forgetting I would need more clearance than in my slim past, I began to slide my body across their laps in an attempt to reach the vacant chair. Well, I made it past Marita, but when I crossed over Becky's lap, the space narrowed, and I didn't. I ended up stuck. Or more accurately, my backside was stuck. And I do mean stuck! Becky had papers, program, and purse in her lap, and somehow I became entangled and Becky became ensnared. The straps of our purses were looped around each other and the chair, tying us securely. We couldn't pull apart the straps or us. I couldn't move sideways or up, and she couldn't move over or back. The more I pulled and tugged, the tighter we became cinched together.

I was now perched on Becky's aerobically thin lap. Both of us were restricted in movement, and to add to our dilemma, we became tickled. The enormous room was fairly dark. That was good. But we were surrounded by thousands of people, and we didn't want to distract them or cause a ruckus. But honestly, we couldn't help ourselves. Becky was laughing so hard she was gasping for air. (That or my added tonnage had knocked the breath right out of her.) I, confused about how I had become permanently affixed to my friend, began to titter. My tittering turned to jostling as my repressed giggles transformed my cellulite body into a human vibrator. I shook so vigorously that I dislodged Becky's papers that had been between us, and they fluttered to the floor. That minute space gave us a little leeway, and with a mighty jerk, I rolled into the empty seat next to my mushed buddy.

We looked at each other, our outfits now askew from our tug-of-war, and we lost it. Tears cascaded down our faces while the arteries in our necks grew alarmingly swollen. Marita looked at us, baffled. She wondered what could possibly have been that funny about our scuffle.

It was one of those times when you not only had to be there, but you also had to be actively involved to understand our reaction. It was unexplainable, but gratefully it was expressible through laughter. Becky and I did gain a wisp of composure but found it necessary to avoid eye contact until after we left the arena, lest we set each other off. Because Becky and I shared deeply an emotion, it added a fun memory to our friendship, enhancing it.

Recently our friends David and Nancy joined Les and me for a northern Michigan, cottage-on-the-lake adventure. They flew in from California for a time of relaxation and fellowship. What we hadn't anticipated was that when the summer residents had moved out of the cottage we were to stay in, Mickey, Minnie, and several namesakes had moved in.

Signs of their intrusion were, *eek*, everywhere. The invading troops had shredded sugar packets, powdered-cream packets, and tea bags for nesting material. They had set up housekeeping in the pots and pans, and one resident was building a condo in a stove burner. She must have decided on a Southwest decor, because she had dragged in a five-inch feather to enhance her surroundings. And of course a profusion of mouse confetti (if you know what I mean) was sprinkled throughout the premises to announce their ownership of the establishment. It was their little way of claiming squatters' rights, and it was obvious they had been doing that very thing.

Well, it's like this, folks: I don't do mice. No how, no way. I was on my way out the door, headed for higher ground, when the others convinced me we could win against these little varmints. Les and David started the cleanup campaign, while Nancy diverted my attention with the beauty of our surroundings. Then we went to town and bought traps. Lots of traps. Scads of traps. And we placed them all around the house.

That evening we were playing Jenga, a nerve-racking game of building a tower one log at a time, when a trap went off. I almost ate my log. The guys yelled, "All right!" Then they gave each other a high-five victory slap, acting as if they had just struck oil. Nancy and I cried, "Oh, no! Yuck!" Then the big-game hunters went to examine their prize. We heard one say to the other, "Oh, cool. Look at how squished he is. Hey, girls, wanna see?"

What is it about guys and guts, anyway? And why do they love to gross out girls? Talk about loony 'tudes!

The trap snapping continued throughout our four-night stay. The guys were thrilled at the sound of each snared tenant, and we girls were nauseated. In the mornings, Les would say to David, "We'd better check our trap lines." You would have thought they were snaring bear. Afterward, David and Les were sorry they hadn't taken a picture with all their prey dangling between them from a clothesline. They really are a couple of Mouseketeers.

Despite my passionate dislike for those little fur balls with feet (the mice, not the guys), we had great fun. In fact, I'm almost certain that without the little creature-feature, we wouldn't have had such a hilarious adventure. Although . . .

David, Nancy, Les, and I took a trip out east two years ago, staying at bed and breakfasts, seeing the breathtaking autumn scenery and eating ourselves silly. The farther east we traveled, the more signs we noticed alerting us to moose traffic. Other than Bullwinkle, I'd never seen a moose up close and personal. We were all vigilant in hopes of being the first to spot a moose. Then one day David suddenly let out a yelp. "A moose! A moose!" he repeated in his excitement. His flailing arms pointed back to a road we had passed.

Les, who's always up for an adventure, did a dramatic U-turn and headed pell-mell for the sighting. He careened the van head-long into the road, and there, facing us, was the biggest, fattest barrel you'd ever want to see. Did we ever laugh! Oh, my, all our sides were splitting. Well, David wasn't laughing quite as hard as the rest of us. So for the remainder of the trip, we took turns yelping at barrel sightings just to make David feel better.

Now that I think about it, it wasn't the mice or the moose that added to our vacations. Instead, it was our loony 'tude friends who make fun a part of their everyday lives.

Have you ever noticed how some people seem to have a greater capacity for fun and laughter than others? Do you think it's in the genes? Or do you think they purpose to find the good, the positive, and the humorous? Hmm, it might be worth a try.

20

Grati-tude

(grat′ e tōōd) n.

Dictionary's definition:
Thankfulness.

Patsy's definition:
Upward tilt of the heart.

'TUDE-OMETER

The top four things mentioned when you ask folks what they're most thankful for are faith, family, health, and friends. I say "Amen" to that list. And I would add another favorite that causes me to sport a 'tude of gratitude: seasons.

My senses are activated in autumn. I love the visual splendor of the landscape, the crunchy sound of leaves underfoot, and the crackle of the fireplace dancing in amber delight. Every fall, I drown my innards in fresh apple cider and then fill my face with homemade pumpkin pie. Yum. My cotton gauzes and seersuckers are replaced by my corduroys and cable knits as I prepare for frosty mornings and chilly evenings. My energy level is at its peak during this exhilarating time of the year.

My heart is renewed in spring. I take great delight when, through the lingering snow, the daffodils press their bright yellow faces of anticipation. The gardens are quickened, as is my hope. Just as the frozen soil is warmed by the sun for productivity, so my resistant heart softens in the Son's light for fruitfulness. Spring is winds, wildflowers, wonderment, and whispered promises. My vision is expanded in spring as I watch the warmed earth unfold its fragrant bouquet.

My stress is soothed in summer. The pace of the days allows

sanity to seep back into my crowded life. Porch swings, lemonade, baskets of daisies, and strolls through town are some of the casual dividends of this gentle season. Chats over fences, songbirds' serenades, open windows, a nap in the sun—all bring strength back to my weary soul. My mind is mended in this mellow season.

My spirit celebrates in winter. A snowy-white carpet covers my backyard, showcasing silhouetted trees with barren limbs raised in praises. I, too, have little to offer the Bethlehem Child besides my arms raised in gratitude as I think about our world, a frigid land thawed by heaven's Light. The frozen sleep of this season prepares us for spring's revival. My life is instructed by winter's necessity as death gives way to resurrection.

The dailyness of life is filled with seasons, too. We feel winter's blast when relationships seem biting and cold. A mom told me her son had become dependent on cocaine, and with the addiction, their weak relationship withered. Her heart ached with grief over the icy year and a half until her son's destructive journey changed seasons. Through his recovery, his brokenness melted his heart and made room for tenderness, gentleness, and gratitude. Like a spring revival, their mom-and-son relationship moved past their winter of adversity. But the mom is quick to point out that without the bitter winter, there could not have been a blessed spring.

My friend Lana was deserted by her husband and left to figure out a solitary future. During the painful process of establishing her life alone, she would take long walks. Every day, she passed a home with a fence full of cascading roses. One day, the roses' sweet fragrance and beauty captured her undivided attention. As she continued her walk, Lana whispered to the Lord that she wished she could have roses like those. She knew that was unlikely since now she had no one to bring her flowers and she wasn't a gardener.

Weeks passed. Then Lana's friend Penny called and offered her a slip from her great-aunt's flower beds. Lana resisted the offer, knowing how unsuccessful she had been at growing flowers in the past, but Penny came anyway and planted the cutting. In the busyness of all the changes in her life, Lana forgot about the new planting. Spring turned into summer before she walked into her walled-in backyard and discovered that the cutting had flourished. The plant had produced trailing fragrant roses just like the ones for which she had longed. Lana was filled with gratitude for the visual expression of the Gardener's care. Spring unfolded the first signs of hope in a rosebush, which was followed by a summer profusion of His provision.

One year brought a different kind of summer to Michigan, a summer of drought. I remember the country road we lived on formed great walls of dust with every passing vehicle. Flowers were stunted and struggled to open against the searing sun. Bluebirds encircled our birdbath, while flocks of other birds waited on nearby telephone lines for their turn to drink and splash away the heat. Water was restricted to indoor use only, which caused the parched grass to brown underfoot. It was the driest summer I had ever experienced.

The first signs of fall brought relief in the form of nippy breezes and moisture-laden clouds. The thirsty land drank deeply of the cool rains and then responded with brilliant autumn colors. Even the grass greened, enhancing the display.

One friend likened it to a drought in her life when she had suffered a miscarriage. She had waited so long in hopes of conceiving and then lost the child of her heart. She was devastated. Following her loss, her relationship with the Lord felt like a desert, barren like her now-vacant womb. Parched by her depression, she felt alone and lost.

After a long season of wandering in her pain, she began to voice her anger and deep disappointment toward the Lord and herself. That was when she noticed the first signs of change. She felt within her a stirring, not in her womb but in her heart. Color began to return slowly to her life. Relationships mattered to her again. Her energy level improved. And seeing other people's babies no longer caused her such piercing pain. She eventually became aware of the Lord's gentle hand guiding her out of the dry land of loss into an autumn of acceptance.

As her pain level decreased, her understanding increased. She realized the Lord had never left her; like a parent with a sick child, He had remained at her side, waiting for the fever to break. She told me her grief eventually colored her life with compassion and her lips with counsel. She no longer offered easy answers to the hard questions of those who suffered. And most of all, she became thankful for a God who waits with us and walks with us throughout our changing lives.

Rain, sleet, snow, hurricanes, or floods, our Season Maker remains consistent, steadfast, faithful, and available. How grateful I am for the changes of all the seasons!

21

Inner 'Tude

(in´ er to͞od) n.

Dictionary's definition:
Secret chambers.

Patsy's definition:
Undisclosed contents.

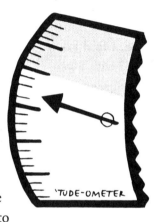

'TUDE-OMETER

A young woman approached me with a little, black box in her hand when I finished a presentation at a conference. "You've made me laugh," she said, "and now I want to give you something to make you laugh." She handed me the box and instructed me to push a series of buttons.

Each button I pressed had a high-pitched woman's voice screeching out some parental instruction: "Stop it!" "I said, stop it!" "You're going to poke somebody's eye out with that thing!" "You broke it; are you happy now?" When you pushed a master button, the woman proclaimed all four statements in a row like an irritating recital. The woman's cantankerous attitude and her nails-on-chalkboard voice bored a hole right through one's nervous system.

I played the box for the hotel clerk and the waitresses, and I even held it next to the microphone and pushed the buttons for the conference audience. Everyone laughed. I had a great time playing it throughout the airport and for the flight attendants on my trip home. Once home, I played it for my son and his girlfriend. She tittered and said, "Why, she sounds just like you."

Funny thing—I stopped laughing. "Oh, really?" I said at a pitch one tone short of shattering glass.

Suddenly the box didn't seem so entertaining. Up to that point, I had chuckled every time that cranky mom with her shrill voice had given a command. Now it had become, well, personal.

Isn't it enlightening to see yourself through someone else's eyes? Sometimes I've been blessed and encouraged by the perspective of others, and sometimes I've been startled and even temporarily shattered. I find I don't always see myself as I actually am but instead how I wish I were or how I mean to be.

My friend Lana, while shopping at an antique store, picked up an old book on graveyard humor, *Chuckles in the Cemetery*, by William Pellowe. It was full of old quotes from tombstones written by people who knew the deceased and who had left their evaluations of the individuals carved on the headstones for future generations. Whoa, now that's scary! Can you imagine what some people might say about you?

Look at what someone wrote on poor George Hotten's gravestone:

Hotten

Rotten

Forgotten

Certainly succinct. Either George didn't make a lot of points with people in this life or his mother-in-law wrote the comments during a gall bladder attack.

Evidently this next inscription was written by someone who lived close enough to Obadiah and Ruth to have experienced the dynamics of their relationship, for that person wrote:

Here lies the body of

Obadiah Wilkinson and

Of Ruth his wife.

"Their warfare is accomplished."

In 1714, Ann Marr, the wife of the parish clerk, passed away, and

someone (the clerk perhaps?) had this engraved on her stone:
> The children of Israel wanted bread,
> And the Lord he sent them manna
> Old Clark Marr wanted a wife,
> And the devil he sent him Anna.

But then Sarah didn't fare much better:
> This stone was raised by Sarah's lord,
> Not Sarah's virtues to record,
> For they're well known to all the town,
> But it was raised to keep her down.

I guess Sarah's hubby had wearied of hearing her rehearse her own inner goodness. Well, perchance Anna and Sarah can commiserate one day with this man's wife:
> Within this grave do lie,
> Back to back my wife and I;
> When the last trumpet the air shall fill
> If she gets up, I'll lie still.

To see how others see us is to risk obtaining more information than we may want. Sometimes I find the Lord will send someone into my life to be a mirror, to help me face what I'm really like. Have you ever been aggravated by traits in another person, only to find out you had those same qualities? I hate when that happens.

There was the time I was scheduled to speak at a conference in the Southwest. I had been ill the night before, and I was still weak and limited to a diet of soda crackers. I was met at the airport by a woman, Isabelle, from the staff of the retreat center. She was carefully dressed in a three-piece, pin-striped suit and wore her long, red hair in a neat braid. While her appearance was orderly, she seemed preoccupied and in a big rush.

As we hurried to her car, Belle informed me we would need to stop at her home to pick up her luggage for the weekend. I was surprised she hadn't brought it with her, since we still had a long drive ahead of us. On the way to her home, Belle told me she would first need to stop at the bank where she worked to take care of an unfinished transaction. At that point, I started to feel a little concerned about our timing, but I was too weak to say anything.

We were in the fast lane on the freeway, traveling at the speed of light, when Belle said, "Uh-oh, there's our exit." Having released that abbreviated traffic bulletin, she then swerved across three lanes of traffic, darted down the exit ramp, and squealed to a halt at the stop sign. I thought I was going to lose my crackers.

After stopping at the bank, we finally made it to her house. There she announced she had to go grocery shopping so her family would have food while she was away. She invited me to go along, but, funny thing, I didn't feel up to the ride. I reminded her of our timetable, but she assured me we would make it to the conference without a hitch.

When Belle returned from the store, she put away the groceries, and then she admitted she hadn't packed yet and disappeared down the hall. Finally she reappeared, suitcases in hand, and we headed for the car. I climbed in the front seat, and in a few minutes she slid in under the steering wheel and stared straight ahead. She didn't start the car; she just stared. After several silent moments, I asked, "What's wrong?"

Still looking straight ahead, Belle stoically replied, "I just locked the car keys in the trunk." We went back into the house and waited an hour and a half for her teenage daughter to bring us another set of keys. By the time the keys arrived, we were too late to make it for my first speaking session.

Belle's daughter's parting words to us were, "Don't rush, Mom, you're already too late to make the session. Just enjoy the drive." Belle smiled as if agreeing with her daughter and then put the pedal to the metal. I was plastered to the seat as we sped down the highway in the inside lane. She was obviously trying to make up for lost time.

Suddenly she uttered, "Uh-oh," just as the car began to lurch as though it had the hiccups. Belle cut across two lanes of traffic, and the car hiccuped to a halt. We had run out of gas. She spotted a service station, but it was on the other side of the six-lane highway. Belle took off running across the lanes and made it safely to the center, where she then had to get down on all fours to slip under a fence. That was quite a sight, since she had accomplished all this while wearing high heels.

I watched from the car as her suit and heels squeezed under the fence. I couldn't decide if I wanted to laugh or cry. I'm certain I was in my physically weakened state so I wouldn't be tempted to commandeer this frenzied woman's car.

She returned with a young man who poured five teaspoons of gas into the tank, allowing us to sputter our way down the road to another station, where we filled up. Once back on the highway (uh-oh), it began to rain. Belle turned on her wipers, and the wiper on the driver's side took one swish across the windshield and flopped down on the side of the car, dangling like a hangnail. She pulled off the road, and we inched our way several miles through the downpour to a gas station where they had . . . no tools. The young man who worked there did, however, run over to a restaurant, borrow an array of knives, and tighten the flyaway wiper.

We returned to the road and headed lickety-split to who knows where—certainly not the driver, who now confessed she was lost. Folks, this definitely was not, I repeat, *not* her day . . . or mine. We did, however, finally arrive—nine hours late. I stumbled into my room that night mumbling unpleasantries.

The following day, I found out that the woman, a widow, had

many extenuating circumstances complicating her life, and I was one of them. In the midst of a multitude of things demanding her attention, I was an (unwanted) addition. She was never supposed to be my driver, but at the last minute, the retreat staff had dumped me into her already overwhelmed schedule. Not wanting to abandon me at the airport, she had tried to fit me into her basket of duties. The problem was she only had a three-egg basket, and she already had 22 eggs precariously piled in it. Then, sure enough, the inevitable happened—the eggs began to topple. Splat. Splat. (Uh-oh.) Splat.

But the real problem with Belle and her egg basket was that I saw myself too clearly reflected. I find that when life gets ahead of me, if I don't make some immediate adjustments, I end up running around like a chicken with her head off.

Now, if you've never seen a headless chicken, trust me, it's not a pretty sight. I watched my farm-raised momma separate a chicken's head from its body with half a dozen circular swings. That was one split chick. The feathered body ran wild, while her head nonchalantly observed from a fence post.

I've had to ask myself why it is that I constantly take on more than I can handle, which leaves me feeling detached and frantic. I'm sure the Lord must grow weary of hearing my emergency, please-get-me-through-this prayers.

I observed Belle's outward behavior, but what I ended up seeing was my own inner condition. I'm grateful the Lord lets us learn from each other and lets us know we're not the only one struggling. That woman was trying to meet everyone's needs, only to encounter one calamity after another. Now, who did that remind me of? It was easier for me to see what she should have done than it is for me to prescribe solutions for myself when I'm in the midst of my own overbooked dilemma—which is more frequent than I care to admit. I, too, take on more than I should and hesitate to use the grown-up word *no* when people try to give me opportunities I just can't afford.

When I met Belle, I thought she was a real Mickey Mouse. Instead, I found out she was a mega-mirror. Had I written her epitaph, I would have simply put, "Uh-oh!" But I realize mine could read, "Uh-oh, too!"

The next time we feel tempted to critique someone's behavior, perhaps we should first ask the Lord if the criticism is just about them or indicative of us. We must own our crankiness, frantic patterns, lack of good judgment, or other fitting insights mirrored by those around us if we're to experience inner growth. I find that when my attitude is supple and I'm willing to learn, He will give me an inner view (sometimes via an outer source) to help me know deep change from the inside out. Then, hopefully, my "Uh-oh's" will become "Oh, I see."

Think-a

(think´ a tōōd) n.

Dictionary's definition:
Headed in the right direction.

Patsy's definition:
Mental agility.

Thoughts can be powerful. Just observe the little train who fueled his tank with "I think I can's." Or consider Barron Lyton, who believed a written thought to be mightier than a wielded sword. Then there's King Solomon, who proclaimed, "As [a person] thinketh in his heart, so is he" (Prov. 23:7, KJV).

'TUDE-OMETER

Oh, brother, am I in trouble! At this stage of my life, I'm given to spells of seesawing from the negativity of narrow-mindedness to the negativity of being a tad morose. And a tad of morosity is like a bad perfume; no matter how little you put on, it still stinks.

It's like the mystery smell in our house. It doesn't arise often, but when it does, it's powerful. We believe it may come from the city sewer lines. (At first we were all suspiciously eyeing each other.) It's almost as if the sewer belches, and we get a backdraft. We spray, use disinfectants, and open windows. But after a while, we don't notice it as much unless we leave, get a breath of fresh air, and come back in.

My negativity (or yours, for that matter) is like the mystery smell in that everyone notices it right off, but no one appreciates it. And the more we're negative, the easier it becomes to adjust to our smelly thoughts, until we don't even realize how bad they stink or how far they've permeated. Negativity is a habit-forming choice and can, unchecked, become a lifestyle. When God's guidelines for our thoughts are followed (see Phil. 4:8), on the other hand, it's like opening a window and allowing a heavenly breeze to waft through.

My six-year-old nephew Nicholas was riding in the car with his mom when he made a dreary announcement: "I hate my life."

My sister was startled but tried not to show it. Calmly she asked, "Well, Nicholas, why do you hate your life?"

He seemed relieved she had asked so he could get it off his chest. He took a breath and sadly reported, "Because of sharks, alligators, and caterpillars."

Cheered to hear it wasn't her, his dad, or his siblings, she probed on. It seems that Nicholas had been fond of sharks, alligators, and caterpillars. But one by one, he had found out they could be dangerous. In fact, just that morning his dad had innocently mentioned that caterpillars can carry germs. Little did he realize the caterpillar was Nicholas's final straw. How much can a fellow take, anyway?

I giggled over Nicholas's mental ruler for hardships. But then I realized I've had similar thoughts—like when my hair acts hysterical, my panty hose generate a run the width of the freeway, or a cold sore the size and shape of Texas sprouts on my upper lip. Then I mentally mumble, *I hate my life.* Yet when my hair settles down, my panty hose are flawless, and my cold sore dissipates, life seems great. My, it sure doesn't take much to throw some of us off, does it?

Here's a list of some of the things that can push my mental dimmer switch: products at the store that aren't priced or are marked, but in the most obscure places. People who write checks in the cash-only checkout lane. Cars that stall in the middle of left-hand turns (especially when I'm driving them). Lids that have obviously been sealed with Super Glue. Stick-on price tags that take off three layers of the product when removed. Window shades that fall off the window every tenth pull. Pens that skip, making our letters look like Morse code. People who bump into me and aren't sorry. Shopping carts with wobbly wheels. Parallel parking. Somebody's gum stuck on my shoe. The parents of impolite children. Boots that leak.

I feel negative just thinking about those things. Oh, that's the point, isn't it? Our mind-set determines our ability to overcome difficulties, and if we can't get past the inconsequential areas of life (like my list), how will we ever deal with the real life-and-death sticklers?

Perhaps we need to think of the irritants of life as our thought aerobics. That would allow us practice opportunities so we'll be mentally strong when the tough stuff hits. Then, instead of clouding over mentally when I see a line at the checkout lane, I could see it as a chance to exercise patient thoughts. If I did that regularly, the next time a heavy-duty issue visited me for an extended time, I'd be more mentally fit and able to handle the hardship with maturity and maybe even grace.

Changing our thoughts to a more positive vein helps improve not only relationships, but also our health. I learned this when I had to go for a series of x-rays because of discomfort in my chest and upper abdomen. I stretched out on an ice-cold examining table with large, looming equipment overhead. I was strapped onto the table. Suddenly, it began to move up and forward until the table and I were standing upright. I was handed two glasses of fluid to drink rapidly. One was, I'm pretty sure, crushed Styrofoam mixed in liquid cement. The other was like cod-liver oil over fizzing pop rocks. I guzzled and prayed it would stay down so I would only have to do this once.

Then the table tipped back and forth, moving me from standing on my feet to almost standing on my head—similar to rides at an amusement park . . . minus the amusement.

Next a doctor came in and asked me what my favorite food was. I found that irritating, since I hadn't had anything to eat except their x-ray cocktail, which would probably require a Roto-Rooter to remove from my system. But to hurry things along, I said, "Banana cream pie."

He looked away and then looked back at me and inquired, "Would you like it with whipping cream?"

For the life of me, I couldn't see the point in his culinary questionnaire. I guess he heard my exasperation as I flippantly said "Sure" to the whipping cream, because he replied, "Mrs. Clairmont, look over your shoulder at the monitor. Those are your insides." He was pointing to the screen, and he continued, "We need to move the fluid you drank from here to here." He moved his finger across the screen to indicate the desired route. "You can cause that to happen if you'll think about a food you enjoy," he concluded.

Fascinated by the idea, I concentrated on banana cream pie (with whipping cream) while watching the screen. To my amazement, the fluid immediately spilled from one area of my anatomy down into another. Then the x-ray technicians finished their filming.

Afterward, it hit me how just thinking about food can create a physical response. That made me wonder what happens inside me when I think resentful thoughts: churning stomach fluids, tightened jaw, pounding temples, strained neck muscles. Does that also mean that when we think up a good 'tude, we could bring peace to our digestive tracts, relaxation to our muscles, and a smooth flow to our circulation? Now, those would be benefits worth working for.

But I find overseeing my thought life far more difficult than observing fluids in my digestive tract. I'm constantly deluged with thoughts both worthwhile and destructive (in the sense that they don't promote goodwill or good health). It's a full-time job to sort through one's thoughts, a challenge with which I need assistance. The good news is we are offered that support via the Scriptures and the monitoring and strengthening ministry of the Holy Spirit.

Our minds, much like television screens, are constantly receiving broadcasts—from others, ourselves, and the Lord. It's our choice which channels we tune into and which we turn off. The more time we spend considering the Lord and His ways, the healthier it is for our bodies (see Prov. 4:22), our minds (see Ps. 119:165), and our character (see Prov. 2:7).

Now, let's see if I understand what I've just said: With the enabling power of the Lord, we can think ourselves into or out of a 'tude. The healthier the 'tude we choose, the healthier we become, allowing us to affect our world in wholesome ways.

I want to think up a 'tude like a little train that takes on a towering mountain; I want to wield a pen that influences minds for good; and I want to have a mind that reflects its Designer in content and conscience. To do those things, it's obvious to me that I'll need to get busy and more conscientiously turn the channel on my screen from majoring in the minors (inconsequentials) to focusing on what matters. *I think I can. I think I can.*

23

Family 'Tudes

(fam′ e lē to̅o̅ds) n.

Dictionary's definition:
Reproducing after our own kind.

Patsy's definition:
Help! I'm my relatives!

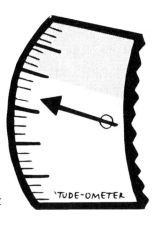

'TUDE-OMETER

My favorite refrigerator magnet reads, "Mom, I'll always love you, but I'll never forgive you for washing my face with spit on your hanky." That statement is funny and effective because most of us have experienced ye ol' spit shine. It's part of our family heritage.

My mom often resorted to the lick-and-rub method to remove smudges from a face or make a cowlick submit. I, too, used the technique with my boys when lack of time or facilities necessitated such an earthy approach. In fact, I think this liquid shine solution should be bottled and sold as an all-purpose cleaning fluid. It removes everything from grease to rust, to chocolate, to smart-aleck smirks. (It's real hard for a kid to think he's clever or cute when his mom is rubbing her spit on his face . . . in public . . . in front of his friends.) We could start a cottage business with this product and call it "Spew and You, a Little Bit of Homemade Happiness." And to think it all began with Momma.

Isn't it amazing what we learn from our families? When I was a kid, I thought that when I grew up, I'd never talk to my kids the way my mom talked to me. Then I grew up, married, had children, opened my mouth, and out came my mother. But I thought she sounded a lot smarter through my lips.

It seems that if we live long enough, we finally understand what our elders were trying to tell us all along. The only problem is now we're the elders trying to give insights to the next generation, and they're looking at us as if we're six slices short of a full loaf. But any way they slice their bread, we know that one day our words will finally become food for thought.

My dad used to tell me, especially when I would ask him for money, that I talked like a woman with a paper head. Recently I related this statement to a friend, and she couldn't stop laughing. When she settled down, I asked her what was so amusing. She said a picture passed through her mind of a woman's head made out of the funny papers. I had heard that statement all my growing-up years, but I never thought it was funny. I realize today what a comical dad I had, but at the time he was, well, just my dad.

One thing he did do that tickled me and my friends was his condensed version of the jitterbug. Because he was slightly knock-kneed and bowlegged, it added to the delight of his little jig. At any given moment, he might, in a 12-inch space, offer his rendition of the Charleston or the old soft-shoe. He was usually dressed in his bib overalls, which added to the comedy. The change in his pockets would jingle, and the toothpick he always held between his teeth would bounce. His dance recital never lasted more than 30 seconds, but that was enough to get us all giggling.

If there was one family 'tude Dad exhibited to me, it was his attitude toward life. He didn't require much to be satisfied: a simple home, a car that ran, some meat and potatoes, and an easy chair. He enjoyed a fishing pole, a water hole, a pocket knife, a harmonica, a crossword puzzle, and Kate Smith singing "When the Moon Comes Over the Mountain."

Simplicity, that's one family 'tude I wish I had caught from him.

My life often seems so rushed and complex, with computers, faxes, portable phones, and answering machines all demanding my time. I think my dad would have been fascinated with today's technology. I can just see him wagging his head in amazement and disbelief. Then he would have gone outside, found a chair in the shade, and whittled a while before he took a nap. Dad was a "Life of Riley" (a hammock between two trees and a soft breeze) kind of guy.

I guess I'm more like my mom in that we're both movers and shakers. And one thing we love to move is furniture. I'm forever changing my house around. I not only move Les's easy chair from one side of the room to the other, but I also sporadically move all the living room furniture into the dining room and vice versa. Les is never sure when he sits down if he should dine or recline.

I definitely inherited my furniture fetish from my mom. Her furniture didn't wear out from being sat on but from being moved about so frequently. She moved her furnishings not only from room to room and floor to floor, but also from house to house. Throughout her adult years, Mom has moved 20 times. It would have been more, but my dad stepped on her apron strings in an attempt to slow her down. Today Mom (who is 80) lives in a senior citizens' apartment building, and guess what . . . she would really like to move (old people get on her nerves), but now *I* have hold of her apron strings.

Speaking of apron strings, my mom always wore an apron when she was preparing meals. I loved it. There's something down-home about that look to me. It smacked of being on duty and being delighted to be there. It was more my mom's attitude than her aproned image, because she genuinely loved to keep a home and care for her family. She always sang as she worked and took time for the smallest details to enhance our home's environment with her special touches.

I'd carry on the tradition and wear an apron today, but my family is concerned it might inspire me to cook. So rather than cause them premature indigestion, I have hung a crocheted apron on our baker's rack. That way, it's a sweet reminder of Mom without being a direct threat to my family that I might go on one of my Betty Crocker capers.

My friend Ann, when she first married, emulated her mom's baking savvy as she rolled out a crust and then filled the pie shell with fruit. She crimped the edges of her crust as she had seen her mom do so many times. She even remembered to preheat the oven, just like her mom.

Well, *almost* like her mom. Ann had failed to check in the oven before preheating it. She had stored a large bag of chips inside.

When she opened the oven door, flames shot out at her like a cannon. Ann grabbed a five-pound bag of flour and, in her panic, dumped the entire contents onto the flames. At first the flames appeared to be smothered. She stood relieved and gazed down at the fluffy, white mountain she had created. Suddenly, like Mount St. Helens, there was a big poof. It frightened Ann, so she dropped the empty bag on top of the eruption, where it immediately burst into flames.

Ann bolted from her apartment and ran to her neighbor's. She almost beat his door down as she screamed, "Fire!" Her neighbor worked the late shift and was sound asleep when Ann accosted his door. Half-awake, he dashed into her apartment and soon had the situation under control. He then pointed out to Ann that had she closed the oven door to begin with, the flames would have been contained and would have put themselves out. (She hadn't had an occasion to learn that from her mom.) As he headed back to his apartment, Ann heard him mutter that he was going to switch to the day shift.

Ann's experience could have convinced her to give up the kitchen and take up croquet, but she had learned more from her mom than how to bake a pie. Her mom had taught Ann not to be easily discouraged, and that experience is an important step to achievement. Ann's mom was a cheerleader for her family. And Ann mirrors her mom's lively spirit and tenacity.

I believe the purpose for families is multifaceted. And one of those sparkling facets is that we might proudly display our positive family `tudes, which we observed and absorbed. Another is that we might remember all the worthwhile ways our first family influenced us so we can "pass them on" in our own homes.

Mega-tude

(meg′ e tōōd) n.

Dictionary's definition:
Greatness.

Patsy's definition:
Big deal.

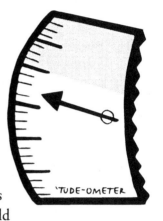

'TUDE-OMETER

Mega-events are exciting to plan for and anticipate, although many times the planning is more fun than the actual event—sort of like the child you buy the new toy for, and after he opens it, you discover he prefers the box. Think of the money we could save if we had just found assorted boxes and wrapped them up to begin with! The kids would be thrilled, we wouldn't be disappointed in their lack of elation at the costly investment, and with the bucks we saved, we could all go to Disney World. Of course, then we would be back to planning another big event, which, in fact, our family did.

A few years ago, Les, Jason, and I went to Disney World on our first vacation in years. We had high expectations for a time filled with laughter and fun. But the day was steamy hot, the park was packed, lines were long, tempers were short, and halfway through the day, a mega-thunderstorm dumped on us. Within minutes, the storm left us ankle-deep in rain as we waded our way to safety and, as a park precaution, the rides were shut down. It certainly was not the day we had dreamed about.

These types of upsets to carefully laid plans tempt us to sport a megatude. We tend to think, *After all our planning, efforts, and financial outlay, this is the big payoff?* We begin to believe we may be better off not having a plan and just letting life unfold in its own quirky way, or to stay home alone and not risk the headache.

Now, I've lived long enough to know high expectations are like hot air balloons. They're beautiful to behold if the elements are cooperative. Otherwise, we end up. . . down . . . and like grounded basket cases, we sit in pools of our deflated dreams.

Yet, even knowing better, we still sometimes set ourselves up to suffer sudden downdrafts of disappointment. Usually my earthward spiral comes from expecting too much from circumstances and people.

I remember as a young teenager being invited to the park one time for a day of swimming with the neighborhood kids. Even though it was a spontaneous event, my expectations were at their peak as I ran about the house to grab a bathing suit, sunglasses, and towel. I heard the knock on the door and anticipated some of my friends had come to get me. When I swung open the door, however, one of the kids hurriedly sputtered, "Sorry, we don't have any room left in the car." With that announcement, she ran to the vehicle, crammed herself in, and off they went on their merry way. I was devastated.

My mom tried to console me without success. I had gone from crushed to fuming, and I was using my fumes to pump up a megatude. Mom caught my attention, though, and defused my ballooning `tude when she said, "Patsy, it's possible the Lord was protecting you from some unforeseen thing. Perhaps you could have been hurt or drowned. We have to trust when things don't go our way that He's watching out for our best interests."

Since that time, my mom's insight has helped me accept a myriad of thwarted events as divinely provisional. Mom's explanation was my first introduction to God's sovereignty, which is an understanding that we have a Divine Director who superintends our every step—yesterday's steps and tomorrow's steps, as well as today's.

Embracing His perpetual care allows us to rest in the confidence that whatever happens, He's not surprised, He hasn't taken the day off, and He's busily at work even in the midst of our darkest nights . . . or our sunniest days while our friends are frolicking at the pool.

Les and I entered our marriage with wild expectations, causing us to take shifts sportin' a megatude. One of Les's assumptions was that I would know how to cook. Can you imagine? I remember his suggesting I make breakfast. I thought, *How ludicrous; we don't even own a toaster.* Les proposed I fix the toast in a skillet. I had never heard of such a thing, so he demonstrated several ways toast could be made on top of and in the oven. I was fascinated but still intimidated by the kitchen. As the years went by, it was my family who became intimidated when I headed toward the kitchen. I guess we could say I wasn't a natural with the culinary arts, although I did find out I was quite good at establishing an artful ambiance.

I love creating a pretty table and preparing an inviting atmosphere: lit fireplace, candle glow, soft music, lively table settings, flared linen napkins, and creative centerpieces. Then I send out for Kentucky Fried Chicken. I know, I know, the Colonel doesn't fit the aura of my efforts, but honestly, it's better than my meat loaf. Mine always seems to be doing the backstroke in a sea of grease (not Greece).

Speaking of stroke, my sister-in-law almost had one when she stopped by my home and noticed I had totally immersed my roast beef in water to bake it. I should have known that was wrong when it gurgled, "Help, I've fallen, and I can't get up!"

I don't think I was meant to cook, but I was meant to converse; not to bake but to blab; not to be a Galloping Gourmet but to have a chatty forte. Once Les was convinced my cooking skills would at best remain at their worst, he gave up his expectations and made reservations. What a relief for us both!

I expected when I married that Les would understand my monthly mood swings. But he thought three rocky weeks out of each month was more like an avalanche than a relationship. He complained just because I whined, "I'm only acting this way because it's the week before." Then the next week I would cry, "I'm only like this because it's the week of." And then, to be consistent, the following week I would assert, "You know I'm this way because it's the week after." That only left us 12 good weeks out of the year.

I finally had to realize Les had never had a menstrual cramp, birthed a baby, or had the blues, and I needed to let him off the understand-me hook. I also needed to obtain help for my erratic hormones and not sport a megatude because others didn't understand me when I didn't understand myself.

Having expectations can be healthy, like being pregnant with hope. But when we become married to our own way, not leaving room for people's imperfections and God's perfect plan, our hope is aborted and we're left grieving.

Expectations aren't wrong so long as we're prepared to shift gears quickly when life takes a twist. Otherwise, if we can't go with the flow, we end up twisted into so many stress-filled knots that we work ourselves into a mega-sized 'tude.

A number of years ago, a hot air balloon landed in our field. The people aboard needed to make some adjustments to their aircraft, but because they made a premature landing, they had to call for drivers to pick them up. They were saddened to change their plan but optimistic that they would be back in the air soon. Perhaps that needs to be our flight plan as well: Fly high when we can (expect the best), land when we need to make adjustments (be prepared to live with change, disappointments, and repairs), and then take off on another day . . . up, up, and away!

Feud
'Tude

(fyōōd′ tōōd) n.

Dictionary's definition:
Ongoing disruption.

Patsy's definition:
Them thar are fightin' words.

'TUDE-OMETER

Like the Hatfields and the McCoys, a lot of feud 'tude-in' is goin' on in this here world. Seems as though we get so married to our own way of thinkin', we don't have room for nobody else's.

Take Les and me, for example. Les and I come from different schools of thought on many topics. Les comes from Bullwinkle's alma mater, What's a Matter U? I attended the notorious School of Hard Knocks. Do you get the picture? We have Hard Head duckin' down in a cornfield and Wise Guy hidin' in the holler, ready to take potshots at anybody (includin' each other) found steppin' on this here land of theirs.

Les and I are both strong-willed people who like being right. Don't get me wrong—I'm not advocating ornery behavior, I'm confessing it. Over the years, Les and I have worked on a more amiable atmosphere, with periodic success. But there are times when we wear each other out by being picky and thin-skinned.

The major issues of life don't seem to be as feud 'tude-in' for us as its constant, minor irritants. For instance, Les likes lots of lights on in our home, floodlight fashion, whereas I'm into the subtleties of candle glow. We seem to go from room to room, canceling out each other's lighting choices. I turn on the dining room lamps that I've strategically placed to add a soft ambiance, and Les walks in and flips on the 300-watt overhead, transforming the room into an interrogation booth. Yes, I want to see what I'm eating, but no, I don't want sunstroke while I'm eating it. Les has accused me of using low wattage to disguise my cooking. Yes. So what's his point? I say, "Whatever works." Besides, if I've already burned the chicken, why regrill it under a blazing chandelier? Anyway, Les and I aren't getting any younger, and like my chicken, we look better under the camouflage of flickering candles. I figure in a couple more years, we'll be eating our drumsticks in the dark.

Lights aren't our only feudin' ammo. There's also the mail. Since Les is retired, he thinks he should be the Pony Express and get the mail every day. But you see, for the first 30 years of our marriage, that was a regular part of *my* day. So now we play mail roulette: Whoever gets his or her hand in the slot first wins the jackpot. If you visit us at noon, enter our porch at your own risk. Neighbors watch from a safe distance as Les and I scramble for position. The mailman has learned to approach our home cautiously in his attempt to remain an impartial participant. He tosses the mail from his saddlebag into our box and then gallops toward the safety of our next-door neighbor's porch.

Once inside our house, the mail-winner gives the loser all the bills, advertisements, and occupant flyers. Of course, that means the winner is often left empty-handed but still wearing a big smirk of victory.

Victory in our home is also won by who has possession of the newspaper. Actually, I don't mind that Les rises first in the morning and brings in the paper. I don't mind that he leaves it spread out all over the couch. I can even deal with the newspaper print permanently tattooed on our furniture. But beware if anyone has tampered with my crossword puzzle! That two-inch part of the newspaper is mine, mine, mine. Do not wrinkle or crumple it. Don't set your coffee cup on it. And whatever you do, don't even think about defiling it with an answer. Them thar' are fightin' words, bub.

For years, some sadist at the newspaper printed the crossword puzzle in the same section as the sports, causing unnecessary strife between Les, the wannabe sportscaster, and me, the wannabe crossword queen. Gratefully, the newspaper repented and moved the crossword and the funnies to a more neutral section, bringing a greater measure of harmony to Les and me.

Added discord, though, can occur between us when we go out to eat—not over our newspaper but over the menu. Les likes to know what I'm going to have before I order. I prefer to order without discussing my decision with him or guests at our table. Don't ask me why, but I just don't want to reveal my choices until the waitress is ready to write them down. Now, isn't that silly?

I find my devotion to my little preferences often indicates the size and condition of my heart. When all is well in my world, I'm more pliable, more amiable, more malleable. But when my preferences become my rights, I tend to be resistant, demanding, and defensive. And if perchance my body is in hormonal havoc the week my preferences are infringed upon, honey, it's feudin' time.

I once threw a hissy fit when Les accidentally tossed out the newspaper before I removed my sacred crossword. You would have thought I had lost my wedding ring instead of a 25-cent, replaceable piece of paper. Besides, I should have been applauding his help in tidying up the house. (Something he had been taught real men don't do.)

Les's dad, Lawrence, was an alcoholic lumberjack who pulled out his own teeth and sewed up his own wounds. Now, that's tough. He had a definite line drawn regarding what he would or wouldn't do as a man. Basically, the way it worked was that if he didn't want to do something, he would make his wife and kids do it.

Les's mom, Lena, was an industrious woman who worked diligently to care for her six children and abusive husband. She chopped wood, built fires in the wood furnace, made her own bread, hung out mountainous loads of wash, and ironed endlessly, including pressing her boys' underwear.

From that background of clearly defined roles, Les then married me. My beliefs and experience were far different from his. I believe a man who helps around the house deserves to live there. I'm into team effort. Besides, two mules can do far more than one.

And one thing this mule doesn't do is iron underwear, though I do wear them (my own, of course). I did, however, light a fire once. I struck the match, and a spark ignited the fuzz that ran down the front of my flannel pajamas. It was quite exciting, but not an experience I cared to repeat. I have, contrary to popular belief, baked bread. It resulted in a loaf that weighed more than me and looked like an oversized hockey puck. Not an experience my family cared to repeat.

Les and I have both had to make adjustments to each other's idiosyncrasies, beliefs, and preferences over the years. And we've learned, in a general sense, that preferences aren't as important as people. Acknowledging and fulfilling our personal desires can certainly be healthy, but putting them ahead of kindness, thoughtfulness, and politeness can be selfish and counterproductive.

If we're gonna go to feudin', we need to 'bide by some guidelines. Number one: Let's fight fair (be kind, thoughtful, and polite). We need to get to the point, not get the person. Number two: Let's fight for what matters—not our rights but righteousness; not preferences but purity; not even beliefs but blamelessness.

Shucks, y'all, we need to lay down our feudin' 'tudes (most of 'em don't add up to a hill of beans anyhow) and instead celebrate our kinfolks and our company.

Plati-tude

(plat´ e tōōd) n.

Dictionary's definition:
Trite remarks.

Patsy's definition:
Easy way out.

'TUDE-OMETER

It's not bright to be trite. (Oops, I think I just broke my own rule.) Triteness and brightness are pictures of contrast. Brightness denotes illumination and savvy, whereas triteness suggests being in the dark and clueless. And that's where we seem to come from when we spout easy-isms.

For instance, if one more person tells me "When life hands you lemons, make lemonade," it's not a lemon I'm going to squeeze. When that phrase first started to circulate, I thought it was sweetly motivating. Now it has gone sour. Yes, I get the point, but repetitive cutesy is as annoying as Chia Pet commercials.

"No pain, no gain" is another saying that's beginning to wear thin. It's accurate but aggravating. I know it's costly to grow, but when I'm walking through the challenge of change with perspiration dripping off my furrowed brow, that's not the time to toss a glib quip my way. Trust me.

Can you imagine Noah hanging a sign on the end of his ark that taunted, "No boat, no float"? True as it was, under the circumstances, it would have lacked sensitivity. Or how about Joseph mocking his brothers with a sign dangling from his multicolored cloak: "No coat, no gloat!" Joe was in enough trouble without spouting platitudes.

I realize our sayings aren't meant to be flippant, but like repeated wearings of even the finest garment, they eventually wear out, lose their initial impact, and become downright tacky. There comes a time to hang 'em up, air 'em out, and give 'em up.

I couldn't help but giggle (and wince), however, when I thought about Bible folks spouting some of our well-known sayings. Imagine big boy Goliath skipping out to meet young David and singing, "Sticks and stones may break my bones, but names will never hurt me." Goliath would have been right about the first part but wrong about names not being hurtful. For after his skirmish with David, Goliath was henceforth referred to as "dead." Following his conquest, David could have, in a vain moment, carved on his sling, "Little strokes fell great oaks," "The bigger they are, the harder they fall," or, tackier yet, "Dynamite comes in small packages."

What about these:

The serpent, as he struts in front of the forbidden tree, waves a placard that announces, "An apple a day keeps the doctor away." (Boo.)

Or picture Jesus calling to the drowning Peter, "Sink or swim!"

What about an engraved stone in front of Lot's wife's statue inscribed, "When it rains, it pours." How about "She wasn't worth her salt"? Or worse yet, "Keep a stiff upper lip."

Imagine Sarah, after Isaac's arrival, pounding this notice on Hagar's tent: "Two's company, three's a crowd." And Hagar's response to Sarah over the camp's loudspeaker: "Too soon old, too late smart."

How about Jonah proclaiming to Nineveh, "Shape up or ship out." Now, that would be the kettle calling the pot black.

Actually, all those comments are grounded in some truth—not sensitive or helpful, but accurate. I'm convinced that the knee-jerk response of a quick retort to life's hard questions is one of humanity's besetting sins. We've all been guilty, out of neglect, ignorance, or indifference, of giving a trite answer to someone in crisis. Often it's because we've either not experienced what that person is going through, forgotten our own neediness when we were in a dilemma, or are unwilling to (or can't) invest the time to help another struggler.

Life can be tough, unfair, confusing, and unexplainable. So there, I've said it. Whew, it's finally out. There's just a lot I don't understand about people and life, but especially about God. I feel safest when I understand what's happening in me, around me, and to me, but often life is a big, fat mystery. And I'm no detective.

I proved that when Les and I attended a mystery dinner with our friends David and Nancy. We ate our meals as a story unfolded around us. Performers portrayed characters involved in a crime, and we were supposed to guess who the criminal was. Only problem was, we didn't understand the play, much less figure out the crime or the guilty party. At first I was afraid I was the only one puzzled by the skit, but when we were supposed to vote on who the villain was, I realized everyone was as stumped as I. Yet we all hesitated to admit our confusion lest we be the solitary soul in the dark.

I find that true of life as well. None of us like to feel we don't "get it." Sometimes we feel safer and smarter when we give a quick reply rather than appear answerless. Our human tendency is to select comfort over vulnerability. But life's mysterious ways often force us to choose between being trite or admitting we're lost.

And as scary as admission can be, it's liberating. What a relief it is, when we're asked something beyond our experience or understanding, to be able to simply say, "I don't know"! The other person may initially be disappointed she didn't find the answer she was searching for, but at least we didn't offend her or mislead her. I'd rather hand out the brightness of honesty than a dim platitude any day. Wouldn't you?

When a friend gave birth to a severely learning-disabled child, person after person told her, "My, the Lord must really love you to trust you with this baby." I think those individuals believed that was a loving statement, but for this woman, in the throes of her shock, grief, and adjustment, it only increased her pain.

Perhaps what we need to do when we have no background in a situation is to say to the one suffering, "Tell me what I can say or do that will help you and not add to your pain." At least that way, the person knows we care enough to be involved and that we're being cautious not to complicate his or her plight with platitudes.

I have learned (the hard way, of course) even to be careful of saying, "I'll pray for you." That begins to sound empty when tossed around casually and constantly. It can be a way for us to detach from others and escape their set of difficult circumstances while maintaining our spirituality. A better way to approach people may be, "How can I pray for you?" That question draws us toward them instead of distancing us. And it says to others, "I'm serious about my prayer offer, and I'm willing to listen while you tell me your greatest need."

One of my favorite proverbs is "A word fitly spoken is like apples of gold in pictures of silver" (Prov. 25:11, KJV). That's what I want to offer to others with my words, a treasured investment of lasting value. The key word is *fitly*. Do our words fit the situation, and do they fit the hearer? Are our words meeting that person's needs? Are we arranging our words as carefully as an artist would if he were painting apples of gold in a setting of silver? Perhaps we should think of our hearer as a canvas, our words as brush strokes, and our interchange as our opportunity to create a masterpiece.

When my friend gave birth to her disabled child, many people extended platitudes. My friend learned she needed compassionate support far more than quick answers. People's advice didn't help like people's availability. Some knew to hold her and her husband and let them weep. And a few left healing brush strokes on the canvas of these parents' hearts when they said, "I can't imagine how you must feel. If you need to talk, I'm available. I'll walk with you through this season. I love you."

A platitude or a masterpiece—one is easy, the other takes effort. It's our choice.

Magni-*tude*

(mag´ ne tōōd) n.

Dictionary's definition:
To a large extent.

Patsy's definition:
Know-it-all.

'TUDE-OMETER

When I checked into a hotel to speak for a woman's retreat one day, I was impressed with the beauty of the place. It was obviously a notch above the norm. My lovely room was equipped with lots of amenities . . . and a couple of unnecessities. Seems some sadistic designer decided to include in the bathroom furnishings a digital scale and, worse yet, an oversized magnifying mirror. At this stage of my life, making weight and wrinkle apparatuses available is not the way to brighten my day.

The magnifying mirror, mounted on an extra-long extension arm, reached out at me as if it were in a hurry for the two of us to share a good laugh. Actually, magnifying even a good thing can be, well, too much of a good thing. But there's something about magnifying our imperfections that can be downright discouraging. Magnifiers have no mercy, they're unforgiving, and their memory for details is uncanny.

Oh, no, I think I've just described what happens to me when I make a big deal out of a small offense! If I harp on trivials until they become trials, I unmercifully magnify errors. And I'm unlikely to forget the details of just how the offense happened. Plus I can't see someone else's perspective—or present.

When Les handed me my fiftieth birthday presents, I was eager to discover what wonderful things he had chosen for me. My husband is thoughtful in his selections and pays close attention to what I delight in, so I knew my gifts would be special. I opened the first box, and it contained a Winnie the Pooh night-light. Being a Pooh fan, I thought it was adorable. Les insisted I plug it in and turn it on. So I did. The light was in the shape of Pooh pushing pots of honey in a wheelbarrow. The pots glowed warmly, enhancing the light's charm.

"What's that?" Les said as he pointed to a wad of plastic wrap taped to the wheelbarrow. I pulled the packet free, looked through the plastic, and saw replacement bulbs for the night-light.

"It's bulbs," I told him.

"Really?" he said with a doubtful air.

"Yes, really," I responded, feeling a twinge of annoyance at his tone.

"Well, it doesn't look like the right size to be bulbs," he stated flatly.

So I looked at the plastic more closely, and sure enough, I saw two replacement bulbs. "Well, that's what it is all right," I smugly assured him.

Then Les picked up the night-light, turned it over, and exposed a lightbulb much larger than the plastic wad I was holding. I began to think my assessment was wrong, and I defensively wondered why the big deal was being made about the bulbs anyway. So when Les challenged me again about the contents of the plastic, I wanted to shove him into the wheelbarrow.

To satisfy him, though, and hopefully to prove my point (my confidence was fading), I tried to open the wad of plastic, but it was secured tightly with Scotch tape. I no longer had the patience to mess with the packet (my 'tude-ometer was on tilt), so I tossed it onto the counter and told him if he needed to see inside, he could open the packet himself. Which he promptly did. Inside was not a replacement bulb but a replacement ring. Les presented me with a breathtaking diamond *ring*. I never had a 'tude dissolve so quickly, nor had I ever been more willing to admit my error.

After I settled down from the thrill of my gift, I was amazed to think that I had been so certain I saw replacement bulbs. I was convinced I was right, and even on close examination, I couldn't see beyond my original evaluation.

I wonder if that's how we become narrow-minded, jump to conclusions, and think ourselves into ruts. We become bound to our own small thoughts that are then magnified by our insecurity and our need to be right. And oh, how I love to be right!

"You really goofed with that one," I chided Les one time as I pointed toward the garage. "What were you thinking? No bluebird will nest in that box with it so close to the buildings, next to the circular drive, and only feet away from where we park. And besides that, it's too high."

A week later, a bluebird scout scoped out our grounds. Les had set up four bluebird locations to choose from, not counting the useless one on the garage. Because we had an ideal setting of open fields skirting the property, I wasn't surprised when the bluebird returned a short time later with his bride.

What did throw me, though, was that this featherhead chose the house of havoc attached to the garage. This bird was obviously not a member of the Audubon Society, nor had he read the same bird habitats book I had.

After several weeks of reminding me (that is, *gloating*) of his keen bird sense, Les took me out to the box to prove (flaunt) once again how discerning (smart) he had been. He lifted the top, and inside, the female bird sat breathlessly still. I was amazed she didn't attempt to fly away—that is, until I heard soft, little peeps. Then I realized she had babies tucked under her wings.

I oohed and cooed and ate every word I had cast in Les's direction regarding his bird savvy. The scene was so dear that I didn't even mind that I was the birdbrain. The picture of those chicks pressed next to their mother's heart has nested in my mind. It magnified for me the shepherd's song of security:

"He will cover you with His pinions, and under His wings you may seek refuge" (Ps. 91:4).

When I press in close to the Lord, I feel safe even in my failures. But when I respond out of my own pridefulness, I'm quick to be defensive and unteachable and to overstate my situation. Then, instead of escaping into the safety of His shelter, I find myself tripping over my puffed-up pride.

I wonder if that's how Paul felt when he fell on his know-it-all face on his way to persecute the Christians. Blinded by the piercing light, Paul's course was diverted and his perspective changed forever. He leaned into the Savior, denounced his prideful ways, and began to magnify Jesus, saying, "He is the Son of God."

What a difference it makes when, instead of inflating ourselves or trying to exaggerate the faults of others, we exalt the Lord together! "O magnify the LORD with me, and let us exalt His name together" (Ps. 34:3).

28

Alti-
tude

(al´ te tōōd) n.

Dictionary's definition:
Distance upward.

Patsy's definition:
View from our knees.

'TUDE-OMETER

I'm not into heights. In fact, I'm a little wary of being five feet tall. With that in mind, imagine how I felt when Les and I bought "Big Bed." That's what we dubbed our stupendous bed after it was delivered to our home.

We purchased Big Bed at an expansive, warehouse-sized store. The vast rooms and vaulted ceilings there swallowed up the enormity of the bed, leading us to believe it could easily be tucked into our modest bedroom.

Les and I saw the bed at home for the first time when we had just flown in from a speaking engagement. We had made arrangements for it to be delivered and set up while we were away. When we walked down the hall toward the bedroom and took it in, we literally took two steps back in shock. Actually, I was appalled. Our bed looked more like a boat—no, make that a battleship. Ol' Ironsides had moored in my room. The iron frame, even with its airy cutout design, looked massive in our petite boudoir.

Heightening our growing dilemma was our giant mattress. We had selected a pillow-topped mattress for comfort, not considering the inches it would add to an already overstated predicament.

After moving the bed around, we finally discovered an angle that would allow us and the bed to be in the room at the same time. Now the challenge was for me to scale Big Bed. When I couldn't just fling myself up onto it, I tried running leaps. I would start in the bathroom and speed toward the bed in an attempt to catapult myself heavenward, only to fall short each time. While I wasn't successful at getting onto the bed, I did manage to entertain my husband and sons with my wild efforts.

Finally, my husband appeared at the doorway holding a step stool. I climbed up onto Big Bed, sat down, and started to giggle. I had never been that close to the ceiling (or Jesus) before. Two things immediately concerned me, though: One was nose bleeds; the other was the ceiling fan. I could just imagine sitting up in bed when the fan was on and getting the ride of my life and a Mohawk haircut at the same time.

Eventually, I adjusted to reaching up to make the bed, to the uphill climb to get into bed, and to the altitude after I arrived. Then I realized how much I enjoyed feeling so . . . so . . . *big*. It was as if I were queen and the rest of the room was my realm. That fantasy fizzled fast, though, when I tried, from my new throne, to give some edicts to my family. They laughed themselves silly.

I've noticed there's something about feeling like a big shot that drastically reduces us in size. The bigger I think I am, the smaller I seem to behave. I guess that's why the Lord warned us against haughtiness. In those moments when we've climbed to great heights, He knows we're susceptible to thinking more highly of ourselves than we should.

Some years ago, I spoke for a ladies' retreat. It was put on by a denomination I hadn't been exposed to before, but one I had nonetheless decided was not very spiritual. I was pleased to be invited and felt I would be able to give them spiritual direction. I knew they would benefit from my insights. Much to my amazement, however, I found them to be far more perceptive, insightful, and spiritual than myself. I wasn't the teacher that weekend; I was the student. I went into the group haughty; I left humbled.

Proverbs 11:2 says, "When pride comes, then comes dishonor, but with the humble is wisdom."

We shouldn't confuse confidence and pridefulness. Confidence comes from a healthy understanding of our worth and capability (see Rom. 12:3). Pridefulness comes from an exaggerated misunderstanding of our worth and capability. Confidence is peaceful; pridefulness is puffed up. Confidence gives credit; pridefulness *takes* credit. Confidence acknowledges supreme authority; pridefulness is its own authority.

I remember that as a teenager, I thought it would be wonderful to escape my parents' authority. Little did I realize what a protection their authority was for my naive and prideful heart. In that same manner, I've learned that being under the Lord's authority protects me—even from my haughty self. When I bend my willful knee before the Lord, He extends to me, like a loving parent, shelter and strength. "The name of the LORD is a strong tower; the righteous runs into it and is safe" (Prov. 18:10).

I ran to a tower once on a Boy Scout reservation, but it wasn't very strong, and neither was I. My friend Edith and I had taken a stroll down to the lake. We came to a towerlike structure with a seat on top for a lifeguard. I decided to scale it, and as I climbed, I informed Edith about some decisions I had made in regard to my future. She cautioned me against being so adamant about my tomorrows. She also wondered if I was sure I wanted to climb the rickety tower. "No problem for me," was my certain reply.

As I ascended onto the chair, I looked down for the first time. That was a mistake. I had more altitude than I knew how to handle. My heart started to do flip-flops, my stomach felt strangely unfamiliar, and a frozen fear descended on me.

Edith, aware of my predicament, began to talk to me gently and reassuringly. She then climbed partway up the ladder and offered her hand. I haltingly moved to the platform's edge and inched my wobbly leg down onto the first rung. Edith supported my foot with her hand to give me the courage to make my next shaky move. Gradually, I made it back down.

If you saw the tower, you would probably laugh at my terrified reaction, for it was fairly modest in size. But you couldn't have convinced my traumatized body or erratic emotions that I hadn't been perched atop the Eiffel Tower. Perhaps that's why Proverbs says "the righteous runs into it [the tower]" and not "on top of it."

On the walk back home that day, I released (again) the tight mental grip I held on my future. I remembered (again) I wasn't ultimately in charge. And I acknowledged (again) that only One should be high and lifted up, and only One can truly guard our lives.

Speaking of guarding, my friend Naomi learned she could neither guard nor control her husband's choices when he became involved with another woman. Naomi had believed her marriage was a model to be emulated. She and her husband had been untouched by hardships and appeared to be the "Cleavers" in their church and neighborhood. But even though she had been approachable, hurting people often failed to connect with her emotionally. Naomi didn't flaunt her family success but rather wore it smugly and mentally criticized others for not having a better grip on their relationships.

Her carefully ordered world fell apart, however, when she discovered her husband had been in a long-term affair. Naomi was devastated by her sense of betrayal. But equally difficult for her was giving up the perfect family picture she had so painstakingly painted.

Eventually, Naomi not only owned her imperfections and her

family's, but also she and her husband worked through the betrayal and infidelity to experience deep relational healing. Now she's the first to confess her proud heart (feeling self-righteous) and judgmental spirit prior to the adultery. She knows her husband's behavior was sin, but she also realizes her attitude of superiority toward others had been wrong. Today, people are drawn to Naomi during times of crisis and find they experience empathy and acceptance in her presence.

To gain altitude, we often need an attitude adjustment. That seldom happens when we're strutting, but it usually occurs when we're kneeling. From that low position, when we are contrite before the Lord, He lifts us up.

"Humble yourselves, therefore, under the mighty hand of God, that He may exalt you at the proper time" (1 Pet. 5:6).

(to͞od´ care ē erz) n.

Dictionary's definition:
Vessels of grace.

Patsy's definition:
Sportin' His Spirit.

A young girl climbed into the seat next to me at an airport recently. She informed me her name was Victoria, and she had been named after a queen, but I could call her Tory. She studied me for a moment and then asked if I knew my name. How astute of

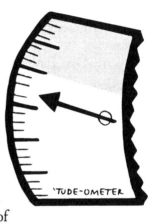

'TUDE-OMETER

her to realize a woman of my age might not have kept track of such weighty information!

I was immediately smitten by this bright-eyed youngster. She was definitely a `tude carrier of the finest kind.

Tory regaled me with one story from her life after another. Yet only once did I detect a slightly contentious `tude. That came when she mentioned a classmate, Theresa. Tory's brown eyes rolled from side to side even at the thought of this girl. It turned out Theresa had stolen two of Tory's boyfriends.

Then a small smile lit up Tory's face as she related that her mom had told her two words she should say to Theresa if she ever bothered Tory again. I wasn't sure it was safe to pursue this insight, but before I could decide, Tory clued me in. She said Theresa came back and tried to steal her best friend, and Tory told her to "bug off."

Trying to hold back a major snicker, I asked Tory if those words had worked.

"Yep," she said. "Theresa never bothered me again."

I couldn't help but think how simple life would be if we could rid ourselves once and for all of negative elements by simply saying, "Bug off." How about "Bug off in Jesus' name"? It's sort of a modern version of "Get thee behind me, Satan." Well, perhaps not.

It's so tempting, like Tory, to want to "give it" to someone who crosses us. But what are we giving them? Yep, our 'tude. Sometimes it's tricky to tell if we're establishing a boundary or generating a 'tude barrier. Boundaries help educate people in how their relationships with us can be amiable. Meanwhile, feisty 'tudes alienate others from us, preventing closeness.

It's gracious of the Lord to supplement our education by allowing us to be a part of each other's lives. I find my involvement with others often squeezes out 'tudes I didn't even realize I had. I know someone else can't bring out of me something that isn't already there. (Phooey.) We have both negative and positive potential, and often that potential is revealed as we interact with others. This revelation, whether jolting or pleasing, presents us with a more accurate assessment of who we are, which then helps us decide who we want to become.

I passed a mirror the other day and glanced toward it, only to see an essence of my father on my face. It startled me, for I've always thought of myself as looking like my mom.

Even if I wanted to, I can't do a lot, short of surgery, to alter my physical appearance. But I can enhance my outer look by my inner attitudes. We're instructed by the apostle Paul to "have this attitude in yourselves which was also in Christ Jesus." Paul went on to define Jesus' attitude. The Lord "emptied Himself, taking the form of a bond-servant" (Phil. 2:5, 7). Jesus displayed a servi'tude.

A young child will one minute beg to help and the next minute plead to have. A sign of growth is when we increase our "help" `tudes and decrease our "have" `tudes. We learn to relinquish our right to call the shots and be in control so we can become more like Christ, to empty ourselves so He might fill us.

My secretary, Jill, remembers going one summer day to Lake Michigan with her husband, Greg, and some friends. The weather was bright, but the winds were brisk. The whitecaps were invitingly exciting. Greg and Jill waded out into the water, but within a short time, she felt intimidated by the threatening waves. She was now in over her head, and in a frantic move, she swam for a nearby buoy and clung to it.

Greg allowed the suddenly-fierce waters to push him back toward land. But Jill refused to let go of the buoy, even though the water was rapidly rising around her. Greg repeatedly yelled to Jill and begged her to let go and allow the waves to carry her to the beach. She persistently held on until she realized that if she didn't take the risk and release her grip, she would drown. In a terrifying moment, she thrust herself toward shore. The turbulent waves took her to safety.

That's how it feels at times to give up our ways and submit to the Lord's—scary and threatening. Yet that act of relinquishment will deliver us from clinging to our negative attitudes and pull us to the safety of His ways. And that brings us full circle, back to our opening chorus:

> "Change my heart, O God
> Make it ever true.
> Change my heart, O God
> May I be like you."

As we change, instead of sportin' a `tude, we can sport His Spirit and become `tude carriers of the finest kind.

Take a Lighthearted Look at Life . . .

with these other books by Patsy Clairmont!

I Love Being a Woman

Join Patsy on a whirlwind tour of women in the Bible that we can learn from today: Esther, Ruth, Abigail and more. Weaving wisdom in alongside her witty observations, Patsy celebrates the unique qualities that make womanhood wonderful. Paperback.

Normal Is Just a Setting on Your Dryer

All of us have things about ourselves that we're not too crazy about. But once we start the comparison game, we wind up in an endless cycle that leaves us all wet! Packed with more of Patsy's side-splitting stories and anecdotes, this best seller is perfect for anyone stuck in the rut of trying to measure up. Paperback.

God Uses Cracked Pots

How does God best reveal Himself in us? When we allow His light to shine through the broken places of our lives. With many hilarious and a few embarrassing tales of a self-proclaimed "cracked pot," Patsy Clairmont encourages readers to take themselves a little less seriously and enjoy life to the fullest, as He intended. Paperback.

.   .   .

www.patsyclairmont.com